NEO-CLASSICAL FURNITURE DESIGNS

A Reprint of Thomas King's "Modern Style of Cabinet Work Exemplified," 1829

THOMAS KING

With a New Introduction by
THOMAS GORDON SMITH
Chairman, School of Architecture,
University of Notre Dame

DOVER PUBLICATIONS, INC.
New York

Bibliographical Note

This Dover edition, first published in 1995, is an unabridged republication of the work originally published in 1829 and expanded in 1835. A copy of the "Second Edition, with Considerable Additions" (H. G. Bohn, London, 1862) owned by the University of Notre Dame was used for the 100 plates and the "Descriptive List of the Plates" reproduced in this volume. In the 1862 edition, the original 72 plates of 1829 and the 28 supplementary plates of 1835 were reorganized into a logical sequence of images based on furniture type, although no changes were made to the pre-Victorian designs.

The title page and "Address" reprinted here are taken from a copy of the 1829 edition owned by the University of Notre Dame. The Introduction by Thomas Gordon Smith has been specially prepared for this edition.

Library of Congress Cataloging-in-Publication Data

King, Thomas.
  Neo-classical furniture designs : a reprint of Thomas King's "Modern style of cabinet work exemplified," 1829 / Thomas King ; with a new introduction by Thomas Gordon Smith.
    p.   cm.
  ISBN 0-486-28289-9 (pbk.)
  1. King, Thomas—Themes, motives. 2. Furniture design—England—History—19th century. 3. Furniture, Neoclassical—England. I. Smith, Thomas Gordon. II. King, Thomas. Modern style of cabinet work exemplified. III. Title.
NK2542.K5A4 1995
749.22—dc20   95-15908
                                                                                               CIP

Manufactured in the United States of America
Dover Publications, Inc., 31 East 2nd Street, Mineola, N.Y. 11501

THOMAS KING

BRITISH AND AMERICAN FURNITURE DESIGN OF THE 1830S

THOMAS GORDON SMITH

IN RECENT YEARS, many images from furniture pattern books by Thomas King have been used to illustrate monographs on British cabinetwork of the second quarter of the nineteenth century, yet King's biography and bibliography have not received much investigation.[1] Edward T. Joy, the scholar who most sympathetically chronicled the design of mid-nineteenth-century English furniture, noted that King "remains a shadowy figure."[2] In many ways, the shadow was cast by disdain for the period when King flourished, an attitude expressed in 1962 by Elizabeth Aslin, author of *Nineteenth Century English Furniture*:

> During the years from 1830 until about 1860, between the Regency and the high Victorian periods, general taste and design in all forms of house furnishing were at a particularly low ebb . . . the complete lack of interest in furniture design was reflected not merely in the dearth of pattern-books but even in the unprecedented depths to which prices [for eighteenth-century furniture] sank . . . ."[3]

Aslin's assertion about pattern books is untrue because the period was actually rife with publications in the genre. A search in British and American libraries reveals that Thomas King was a particularly heavy contributor, having produced 28 pictorial books between 1822 and 1848. King distributed his books in unbound parts: whether bound or loose, they must have received rough handling in cabinet or upholstery shops, because few survive. Ten of the titles have not been located, but they are known from advertising pamphlets bound at the back of other books. Eighteen titles still exist, and a number of them are preserved in unique copies. Although the books

were rarely imprinted with a date, a hypothetical chronology of King's titles is presented based on the occasional imprint, dated advertising supplements, reviews of the books and interpolation from dated watermarks.[4]

Fourteen of King's books illustrate furniture designs in the Grecian, Gothic, Old French [Rococo] and Elizabethan styles. One book concentrates on an architectural subject by featuring designs for shop fronts.[5] The remaining 13 illustrate the design of upholstery and focus on hangings and draperies for windows and beds. All but one of the 28 titles, *The Upholsterers' Accelerator*, bear the name of Thomas King as author.

The Modern Style of Cabinet Work Exemplified was first published in 1829 and became the most popular of King's furniture titles. It went through numerous reprintings until the surprisingly late date of 1862 and was influential beyond Britain—particularly in the United States. This introduction will emphasize both the direct and the more subtle influences *The Modern Style* had on cabinetmakers in America as early as 1834. Ironically, King's impact on furniture design is more clear on this side of the Atlantic than it is in his native country.

BIOGRAPHY

Little is known about Thomas King's life. Although the names of his parents and his exact birth date are still obscure, there are indications that he was born about 1790, the son of an upholsterer and paperhanger named William King. Until 1825, William King's address was 26 Duke Street, Bloomsbury. Thomas King noted this street number on an otherwise unidentified plate from one of his earliest publications.[6] William King may have been the "upholsterer of forty-five

---

[1] See Appendix I for a bibliography of references to Thomas King.

[2] Edward Joy, "Introduction," *Pictorial Dictionary of British 19th Century Furniture Design* (Woodbridge, England: Antique Collector's Club), 1986, p. xxii. This useful book is a compendium of images taken from nineteenth-century British pattern books arranged by typological categories. It surveys designs for sideboards, for example, from 1802-1910. The book employs a number of titles of the period 1830-60. Aside from books by Thomas King, other sources include Peter and Michelangelo Nicholson, George Smith, John Taylor, Richard Brown, J. C. Loudon and Richard Bridgens.

[3] Elizabeth Aslin, *Nineteenth Century English Furniture* (New York: Thomas Yoseloff), 1962, p. 27.

[4] See Appendix II for a list of titles by Thomas King with hypotheses of publication dates.

[5] David Dean, *English Shop Fronts; from Contemporary Source Books, 1792-1840* (London: Tiranti), 1970.

[6] This single plate is preserved within a bound volume that consists of signatures from a variety of Thomas King books, unofficially titled *King's Designs for Cabinetmakers and Upholsterers.* It is located in the collection of the Grand Rapids Public Library, Grand Rapids, Michigan.

years' experience" referred to on the title page of *The Upholsterers' Accelerator*, and therefore its author.[7] This book was recently reprinted because its explanations and clearly executed engravings provide valuable insights into the methods and tastes of the mid-1830s.[8]

Thomas King's name first appeared in a London business directory of 1811 as a "spring curtain manufacturer and French plate worker" in Drury Lane.[9] Although he was never listed as a cabinetmaker or upholsterer, he published his first known collection of designs in 1823, *Household Furniture*, calling himself, "T. King, Furniture Draftsman." King continued to be listed in the directories

associated with the business he had established in spring curtain and French plate work, with occasional references to a brass foundry. In 1833, King was listed as the partner of James Phillips, a brass founder who became independent by 1838. Although these occupations place King in the craft and manufacturing milieu, it was not until 1835, after publishing at least twenty titles, that King listed himself as a "publisher of designs for household furniture." In 1839, he was listed as a "furniture pattern drawer"[10] and in 1841, simply as "publisher."[11] He died about 1842 and several titles were brought out posthumously, imprinted "the late T. King."

Some have speculated that Thomas King was not a designer but simply compiled designs accomplished by others. John Claudis Loudon, himself a publisher of furniture designs, reviewed several books by King between 1834 and 1839 in *The Architectural Magazine and Journal*. Loudon's review of *The Cabinet-Maker's Sketch Book of Plain and Useful Designs* reveals his assumption that King's designs were borrowed: "Not a few of the designs resemble those published in our *Encyclopædia of Cottage and Villa Architecture and Furniture*; the reason, doubtless being, that both have been obtained from the same source; viz. the portfolios or warehouses of the principal London manufacturers."[12]

---

[7]Gail Caskey Winkler suggests that Thomas King might not be the "author."

[8]Gail Caskey Winkler, "Introduction," *An Analysis of Drapery* by James Arrowsmith [1819] and *The Upholsterers' Accelerator* by Thomas King [1833] (New York: Acanthus Press), 1993, pp. v–xxvi.

[9]*Kent's Original London Directory*, 1811, Guidhall Library, London.
Donald Fennimore, Curator at Winterthur Museum, kindly provided information on French plate work: "a narrow specialty in which thin sheets of silver were applied to brass objects with pressure by hand. This was used for tankards and table equipment and also possibly ornamental mounts." Fredrick Bradbury, *History of Old Sheffield Plate* (London: Macmillan Co., Ltd.), 1912, pp. 96–97.
A description of spring curtains is provided in J. C. Loudon's *An Encyclopædia of Cottage, Farm, and Villa Architecture and Furniture* (London: Longman), 1833, Vol. I, pp. 341–342: "A great improvement in this description of blinds has been made by forming the roller of a tin case that encloses a spring, which acts so as to turn the roller, and to pull up the blind of itself. The best description of this spring roller blind is one improved by Messrs. Barron and Mills, which we shall describe when treating of blinds for villas. Sometimes, instead of linen blinds being plain, they are painted with transparent colours, so as to represent stained glass windows, landscapes, &c. These blinds, while they exclude the sun, admit abundance of light, and are very suitable for staircase windows, or the windows of cottages which have either no view, or one which it is desirable to exclude."

[10]*Post Office London Directory*, 1839, Guildhall Library, London.

[11]*Robson's London Directory*, 1841, Guildhall Library, London.

[12]J. C. Loudon, *The Architectural Magazine and Journal of Improvement in Architecture, Building and Furnishing, and the Various Arts and Trades Connected Therewith*, Vol. IV (London: Longman, Orme, Brown, Green & Longman), August 1837, "Art. IV," pp. 394–399.

1. *Thomas King, commode and glass, first plate from* Household Furniture, Comprising 38 Designs of Utility and Elegance *(c. 1823). (The Metropolitan Museum of Art, Harris Brisbane Dick Fund, 1935. [35.45.6L]. All Rights Reserved.)*

2. *Unknown cabinetmaker, sideboard constructed for the Marquis of Bute, Edinburgh (c. 1820). (The Country Seat, Nettlebed, Oxfordshire.)*

A comparison between Loudon and King images suggests, however, that King displayed the sensibility of a designer and was not a mere copyist. The character exhibited by many of his designs is far more effervescent than those of Loudon's plodding chronicle.[13] Similarities between King's designs in *The Modern Style* and pieces produced by important furniture manufacturers like Thomas and George Seddon, Ball, Forman and Co., Holland and Sons and Gillow & Co. suggest that King at least kept abreast of changing currents.[14] These high-quality manufacturers employed their own designers, but this luxury was not available to the smaller London or provincial cabinetmaker and King's books reflected contemporary trends for the small-scale artisan.[15]

In the mid-1820s, King illustrated a commode and pier glass in *Household Furniture, Comprising 38 Designs of Utility and Elegance* that resembles a British sideboard made about 1820 for the Marquis of Bute for an estate near Edinburgh (Figs. 1 & 2). Both designs have a central storage area flanked by slender columns that define open areas for the placement of vases. Silk curtains provide texture and color and arches reinforce the architectural quality of each cabinet. King did not provide a caption for his plate, but the monumental mirror suggests that the piece was intended as a commode for a drawing room, to be placed against the masonry pier between two windows. We will return to this image and compare it to a more sophisticated example of the type in *The Modern Style of Cabinet Work Exemplified.*

MODERN GRECIAN

The Modern Style primarily illustrates furniture designs that were called "Grecian" in the nineteenth century. These were the outgrowth of the dominant Classical facet of the Regency which had developed from archaeological prototypes published by Charles Heathcote Tatham in 1799 and Thomas Hope in 1807.[16] By the 1830s, the didactic character was less overt and the Grecian designs more synthetic. This phase was further defined by another nineteenth-century term, "Modern," and King's emphasis of this word in his title distinguishes the contents from his later books such

3. *Thomas Hope, center table, from Plate XXXIX,* Household Furniture and Interior Decoration *(1807). (Dover Publications, Inc.)*

as *Specimens of Furniture in the Elizabethan & Louis Quatorze Styles*, which promoted non-Classical designs.

The allusions to Greece and Rome in *The Modern Style* are not only in "the boldest scrolls, or in the massive foliage" and "rosettes, enriched mouldings, ornamental borders" but also in the columns supporting entablatures and pediments. Broad planes and blockish forms provide additional architectonic expression as in the "Dwarf Bookcase" of Plate 69. The architectural character is also apparent in the massive wardrobe of Plate 61, which for functional reasons is as big as a shed. The imitation of ancient marble candelabra bases also adds an architectural quality to tables. The lion paws shown at the bottom of King's Plate 45 are similar to the literal incorporation of a Greco-Roman tripod for a table support introduced by Thomas Hope in 1807 (Fig. 3). In King's plates, the zoomorphic forms of the late Regency are more often abstracted into vegetal scrolls or bun feet like those seen in other examples on Plate 45.

IMAGE AND INTENTION

Drawing was King's most natural medium of expression, and the "Address" printed at the beginning of *The Modern Style* is the only statement of purpose written for any of his publications.[17] King geared these paragraphs to the "Cabinet Manufacturer" and stated that the designs were mostly original. His provocative reference to their blend of English and Parisian tastes makes one wonder what aspect of French design he was

[13]Harvey Ferry and William Clegg, *Signed and Designed,* sales/exhibition catalog (Nettlebed, England: The Country Seat), n.d.

[14]Christopher Gilbert, *Loudon Furniture Designs* (Menston, England: The Scholar Press), 1970.

[15]Pat Kirkham, *The London Furniture Trade 1700–1870* (London: The Furniture History Society), 1988, pp. 100–103.

[16]Charles Heathcote Tatham, *Etchings, Representing the Best Examples of Ancient Ornamental Architecture* (London: Author), 1799; Thomas Hope, *Household Furniture and Interior Decoration* (1807), reprinted as *Regency Furniture and Interior Decoration* (New York: Dover Publications, Inc.), 1971.

[17]*The Upholsterers' Accelerator* of 1833 and its reincarnation as *The Upholsterer's Guide: Rules for Cutting and Forming Draperies* of 1848 share the same introductory text. I believe that the existence of lengthy introductions further distances King from being the author of these books and reinforces the idea that another individual, such as William King, provided the account of professional methods. All subsequent upholstery titles are imprinted Thomas King and none have introductions.

4. *Unknown cabinetmaker, sideboard, England (c. 1835). Mahogany and mahogany veneer. (Author.)*

considering. The influence of French Empire on English design had been acknowledged earlier in the century when Hope cited the brilliant Napoleonic architects Percier and Fontaine as an inspiration. Looking for sources closer to King's period, investigation of 1820s French publications does not immediately suggest that they were his sources for "Parisian" blending. His reference may be a more general comment on the long term impact of the Empire and awareness of contemporaneous French Restauration furniture.

The images of *The Modern Style of Cabinet Work Exemplified* are rendered in the crisp linear format of engravings. Occasional details are shown in elevation, but most designs are presented in perspective with scales for measurement provided below. In some cases, the perspectives are amplified by the chiaroscuro of aquatint to suggest the patterning of wood grain and the depth implied by shadow. Selected images are watercolored and these are consistent from copy to copy. Unfortunately, few of the upholstered pieces are rendered in color, which would be valuable for understanding the vibrant chromatic sensibility of the period.[18]

Although the majority of plates rely on the engraved line, King's intentions for material and finish are described: "many of the plain parts of breadth were intended for rich veneer, finely polished, and . . . in the gilded parts, carving is required only in the boldest scrolls." We should envision the images enriched with the color of mahogany or rosewood. Mahogany would have a riot of variegated crotch grain in which the color

[18]The brilliant upholstery colors favored in the 1830s are well represented in Thomas King's watercolor plates for *Household Furniture, Comprising 38 Designs of Utility and Elegance* and in his many upholstery titles.

of contrasting flames would be enhanced by the glasslike sheen of French polish.[19] The glint of gilt decoration would complement these flat but ebullient surfaces.

The variety of sideboards King presented in *The Modern Style* gives a sense of the levels of expense he offered through his book. Simple boxy types on Plates 52 and 53 have little carving or contour and are contrasted with a mid-level example detailed on Plate 50. A small English sideboard made about 1835 falls midway between these and gives a sense of the character achieved when riotous patterns of grain were applied to otherwise simple geometries (Fig. 4). In the caption for Plates 56 and 57 King indicated, "The plain panels in the centre were

[19]Crotch grain is formed at the lateral branches of the tree where the growth structure of the crotch produces complex and variegated patterns due to the grain running in several directions to reinforce the branch structure.

5. *Thomas Hope, large library or writing table (front and side elevations), from Plate XI,* Household Furniture and Interior Decoration *(1807)(Dover Publications, Inc.); compared with: Thomas Cook and Richard Parkin, sideboard, Philadelphia (1820–22). Mahogany, mahogany veneer, white pine and poplar. (The Baltimore Museum of Art: Gift from the Estate of Margaret Anna Abell; Gift of Mr. and Mrs. Warren Wilmer Brown; Gift of Jill and M. Austin Fine, Baltimore; Bequest of Ethel Epstein Jacobs, Baltimore; Gift of Mrs. Clark McIllwaine; Gift of William H. Miller and Norville E. Miller II; Bequest of Leonce Rabillon; and Gift of Mr. and Mrs. Louis Schecter, by exchange. BMA 1989.26.)*

intended for very fine wood." The relative simplicity of all of these sideboards is apparent, however, when compared to the elaborate "Sideboard Tables" rendered in the aquatint Plates 54 and 55.

In the "Address" King projected how *The Modern Style* might be used: "Considering the clearness with which the Plates have been executed, it is expected that directions in the working parts would be useless, especially as the wood made use of, and the retaining all the ornament, must be optional, or regulated according to the richness required . . . ."[20] This comment acknowledges that the cabinetmaker could employ the designs as he saw fit. The book could be copied from directly, or used in an eclectic way. Some plates required a pick-and-choose method. On Plates 13 and 14, for example, King presented variations on the fulcrum arm that derived from Roman couches. The maker could evaluate a variety of "sofa ends" and substitute one of these motifs for the arms shown in drawings of whole sofas on Plates 9 and 10 or Grecian "Couches" on Plates 11 and 12. The results of this method can be seen in the myriad interpretations of built examples.

BRITAIN IN AMERICA

From the eighteenth through the late nineteenth century, American cabinetmakers depended on British pattern books as sources of fashion and technique.[21] A recently discovered sideboard made about 1820 by the Philadelphia partners Thomas Cook and Richard Parkin was inspired by the front elevation of a writing table in Thomas Hope's 1807 *Household Furniture and Interior Decoration* (Fig. 5).[22] Although Cook and Parkin ignored Hope's mausolean side elevation, their piece's paw feet with wings, corner acroteria and thin slab spanning tower-like piers reflect Hope's ideas. Nonetheless, the American cabinetmakers made characteristic changes when they eliminated surface decorations like the ormolu mounts on the door panels and the lion-head drawer pulls. They enhanced the paradigm by adding freestanding columns to the upper aediculae, but they omitted Hope's stele-like pediments. Hope's engraving provided no indication of wood grain or color, but the artisans employed crotch-grain mahogany veneer throughout. They even applied strips cut consecutively from the same flitch to the slats of tambour doors to preserve the dramatic flamelike pattern of the grain. The difficulty of this technique suggests that the inherent decorative qualities of the wood itself were prized over carving and applied mounts.

During the 1830s, American craftsmen employed *The Modern Style of Cabinet Work Exemplified* in similar ways. Copies of King's books are concentrated in Boston, New York and Philadelphia libraries, and a good deal of furniture from these regions derives from *The Modern Style*. In some cases, cabinetmakers extracted motifs from the plates and then applied them to designs which otherwise retained American typology. Other examples follow King's designs so closely that essentially English furniture was fabricated on these shores. During the 1840s, *The Modern Style* had a less obvious but important influence on the abstract phase of Grecian design.

PHILADELPHIA

A dressing table made in Philadelphia in the mid-1830s illustrates how one component from a Thomas King design could be added to a piece of furniture that otherwise retained an indigenous design sensibility. This handsome "toilet" is one of many associated with Philadelphia cabinet warerooms of the 1830s (Fig. 6).[23] On Plate 74 King presented six options for "Pediments for Bookcases &c." In the version at the bottom, raking coronae meet in scrolls at the apex and terminate at the corners with acroteria, again formed from scrolls. Below the apex, bell-shaped leaves fall in front of what King surely intended to be a wooden tympanum. The cabinetmaker who made the dressing table placed the pediment atop slender columns, but misinterpreted the linear format of the engraving and left the center of the pediment void.

Since it is obvious that the artisan relied on King's plate for the pediment, one might ask if the

[20]Despite this statement, in 1833–34 King published a beautifully lithographed folio, *Working Ornaments and Forms; Full Size*. This must have satisfied a need for some cabinetmakers to imitate a full-size model rather than scale up from small engravings by eye or calculation. The only known copy of this title is at Guildhall Library in London.

[21]A valuable collection of English furniture pattern books has been reprinted over the years by Dover Publications. This includes the 1762 edition of Chippendale's *The Gentleman and Cabinet-Maker's Director*, the 1793 edition of Thomas Sheraton's *The Cabinet-Maker and Upholsterer's Drawing-Book*, the 1794 edition of George Hepplewhite's *The Cabinet-Maker and Upholsterer's Guide* and the 1807 edition of Thomas Hope's *Household Furniture and Interior Decoration*. Thomas King's *The Modern Style of Cabinet Work Exemplified* of 1829–32 fills a gap between these well-known classics and the full expression of mid-nineteenth century British taste in *The Cabinet-Maker's Assistant* of 1853 by Blackie and Son, also reprinted by Dover.

[22]Wendy A. Cooper, *Classical Taste in America, 1800–1840* (New York: Abbeville Press), 1993, pp. 56–57.

[23]The example has been attributed to David Fleetwood by the Art Institute of Chicago because of its similarity to a labeled dressing table owned by David Dunton. Fleetwood may have made furniture or he may simply have had a wareroom from which the products of Philadelphia craftsmen were sold. Several other examples of the same form are associated with the Philadelphia cabinetmakers Charles H. White and Barry and Kirkebaum. All of these individuals are noted in Kathleen Catalano, "Cabinet-making in Philadelphia 1820–1840, Transition from Craft to Industry," *Winterthur Portfolio* 13 (Chicago: The University of Chicago Press), 1979.

Jay Carey, Donald Fennimore and Ike Hay have provided helpful thoughts on this issue.

dressing table as a whole derives from another design in *The Modern Style*. A similar form, which has columns supporting a working surface on which glove drawers flank a squarish mirror, can be seen on Plate 92.[24] This design was imitated by another American cabinetmaker; the proportions suggest that one would sit before the mirror (Fig. 7). On the other hand, the proportions of the Philadelphia piece are distinctly different because the mirror has the vertical aspect of a cheval glass, a configuration never seen in English examples.[25] The Philadelphia dressing table must have been used while standing, thus perpetuating an American type from the Federal period. It could even be said that the misinterpreted pediment unintentionally reinforces the taut Federal aesthetic.

[24]Webster and Parkes, *The American Family Encyclopædia* (New York: Derby & Jackson), 1858, page 300, shows a similar toilet, or dressing table, in Figure 425. The text explains why King's mirror does not have a bottom rail: "As this table is commonly placed against a window for the advantage of good light, if the mirror is placed upon it loose, it is apt to be blown down, and perhaps broken, when the window is left open. The best way, therefore, is to have the mirror and frame to slide up and down by means of balance weights, as in a window sash."

[25]Frances Collard made this point when looking at the comparison.

BOSTON AND SALEM

An upholstered mahogany "easy chair," possibly from Boston, demonstrates a more eclectic method of using *The Modern Style of Cabinet Work Exemplified* (Fig. 8). Instead of taking one image from a plate, the artisan manufactured a composite of three King designs.[26] The legs and overarched back derive from the lower portion of Plate 24, whereas the peaked crest comes from the image above it. The arms, with padded rests, are similar to the lower image in Plate 26. A similar chair is painted in back of a portrait of Daniel Webster presented to the Boston Athenaeum in 1832 (Fig. 9).[27]

Several copies of *The Modern Style of Cabinet Work Exemplified* must have been owned by cabinetmakers in the Boston area because numerous motifs commonly thought of as "Boston" actually derive from Thomas King.[28] A commission in

[26]Ike Hay made me aware of the chairmaker's dependence on King and noted the similarity of the chair to that in Daniel Webster's portrait.

[27]Cooper, *op. cit.*, pp. 247–248.

[28]Page Talbott, "Seating Furniture in Boston, 1810–1835," *The Magazine Antiques*, Vol. CXXXIX, No. 5, May 1991, pp. 956–969.

6. *Attributed to David Fleetwood (act. 1833–37), dressing table, Philadelphia. (The pediment is taken from King's Plate 74.) Mahogany with maple, walnut and mahogany inlay. 84 × 35½ × 20". (The Art Institute of Chicago: Restricted gift of Mrs. Henry C. Woods, 1970.38. Photograph © 1993 The Art Institute of Chicago. All Rights Reserved.)*

7. *Unknown cabinetmaker, dressing table, possibly Boston (c. 1835). (After "A Toilet," seen on King's Plate 92.) Mahogany. (Courtesy, Didier, Inc., New Orleans.)*

8. *Unknown cabinetmaker, easy chair, possibly Boston (c. 1835). (After three images from King's Plates 24 and 26.) Mahogany. (Courtesy, Ike Hay.)*

9. *Chester Harding, portrait of Daniel Webster (standing before a chair modeled on King prototypes) (1828–30, 1849–51). Oil on canvas. (Courtesy, Boston Athenaeum.)*

Salem provides an example of how King's book could serve as a direct model rather than as a collection of discreet patterns for varied application.

In 1834, George Peabody, son of a Salem shipping magnate, hired cabinetmakers Abraham Kimball and Winthrop Sargent to help renovate a fifteen-year-old house for his family.[29] In addition to the task of refinishing doors and woodwork, Kimball & Sargent were commissioned to make furniture for the residence. Receipts for Peabody's transactions with Kimball & Sargent provide an inventory of specific items.[30] Some of these are documented in photographs of the Peabody interiors taken in the 1880s and are immediately recognizable as King designs.[31] Further evidence of the importance *The Modern Style* played in this commission is found in the library of the Boston Athenaeum, where a

copy of the 1832 second edition of the book is inscribed

Kimball & Sargent
Salem

10. *Abraham Kimball & Winthrop Sargent, sideboard, cellarette and dining room chair for George Peabody, Salem, Massachusetts (1834). (These pieces derive from King's Plates 21, 50 and 51.) Detail of a photograph taken between 1882 and 1885 by John Lowell Gardner. (Courtesy, Peabody & Essex Museum, Salem, MA.)*

[29]Kathleen M. Catalano, "Abraham Kimball (1798–1890), Salem Cabinet Maker," *The American Art Journal*, Vol. XI, No. 2, April 1979, pp. 62–70.

[30]Receipts from Kimball & Sargent, Salem, 1834, 1836 and 1837 in the George Peabody (1804–1892) Papers, (manuscript accession #87038), Peabody Essex Museum, Salem, Massachusetts.

[31]Anne Farnam, "Typescript of lecture on the George Peabody archival material." Archives, Peabody Essex Museum.

An 1880s photograph of the Peabody dining room shows a sideboard with a cellarette, or wine cooler, poised between the pedestals (Fig. 10). One of twelve dining chairs stands to the right of the sideboard. The receipts indicate that in 1834 Kimball & Sargent charged George Peabody $75 for the sideboard and $50 for the cellarette while each chair was made for $6.75. Thomas King did not designate any chair designs for the dining room specifically, but parlor and drawing room chairs were shown on Plates 15–18 and comprise the basic type Kimball & Sargent followed. These variations on the Greek *klismos* have back legs and stiles cut in an S-curve that supports a broad tablet for the crest rail. None of King's examples were used as a direct model, but Kimball & Sargent adapted the volutes that terminate in clinging acanthus leaves in the modest "Bed room Chair" on Plate 21 for the crest rails of the Peabody chairs. The anomalous Rococo stay rail does not derive from any of the "Old French Style" images King included. Although the turned front legs are like typical English variations on Roman thrones seen in most of King's versions, the unusual palmettes, set like acroteria over each leg, have no precedent in *The Modern Style*.

The base of the sideboard is easier to identify because it is taken almost unchanged from Plate 50 and a variant "Sideboard Back" is substituted from Plate 56. The sideboard doors are decorated with acanthus sprigs that flower into half-palmettes and these intertwine to create a full palmette, a motif that might be called King's signature. King did not illustrate a cellarette, so Kimball & Sargent created a hybrid based on motifs taken from the sideboard. An easy chair of the sort seen in Figures 8 and 9 occupied a place of honor in the dining room opposite the Kimball & Sargent sideboard and was referred to as "Grandfather Peabody's Chair."[32]

George Peabody may have requested a reserved character for his dining room, but he allowed Kimball & Sargent to be extravagant in his "Yellow Drawing Room." In 1803, Thomas Sheraton stated, "the drawing room is to concentrate the elegance of the whole house, and is the highest display of the richness of furniture . . . ." He suggested that it include "a commode, pier tables, elegant fire screens, large glasses . . . ."[33] In the 1830s in Salem, this type of room still had to measure up to such standards. Receipts from 1837 record that Peabody paid $500 for a "Commode & Pier Table executed in Rosewood with gilt ornaments, marble tops & glass." This elaborate work stands nine feet tall and replicates King's design from Plate 36 (Fig. 11). Its size, rich rosewood veneer and gilding, plus the expansive use of costly mirror, combined to create an expenditure seven times greater than the sideboard. George Peabody's commode and

[32]Clara Endicott Sears, *Early Personal Reminiscences in the Old George Peabody Mansion in Salem, Massachusetts* (Concord, NH: The Rumford Press), 1956, p. 38.

[33]Thomas Sheraton, "Furnish" and "Drawing Room," *The Cabinet Dictionary*, reprint (New York: Praeger Publishers), 1970, pp. 201, 218.

11. *Kimball & Sargent, commode and glass for George Peabody, Salem, Massachusetts (1836–37). (This derives from King's Plate 36.) Pine, gilt pine and rosewood veneer. (Courtesy, Peabody & Essex Museum, Salem, MA.)*

12. *View of the yellow drawing room, George Peabody House, Salem, Massachusetts. Detail of a photograph taken between 1882 and 1885 by John Lowell Gardner. (Courtesy, Peabody & Essex Museum, Salem, MA.)*

glass may be the only example of King's ambitious design ever produced.

Kimball & Sargent changed only a few details from King's plate. The staid anthemion cresting above the cornice was replaced with a more fluid rinceau of acanthus in which the dynamic movement is terminated by lateral acroteria formed by half-palmettes. King's signature of intertwined palmettes at the center could have been taken from a number of images, such as Plates 9, 22 or 83. Another change resulted from either oversight or an effort to make the piece "economical." King rendered the skirting which supports the commode slab as a cyma, following the profile of the ornamental mounts located above each column. By contrast, Kimball & Sargent's skirt is flat.

When the commode is compared to the design shown in *Household Furniture* (Fig. 2), it is clear that King had become a better designer in five years. Practical problems, such as properly attaching the mirror to the commode, are resolved and the overall proportions are improved.

The Peabody commode and glass provides a tangible indication of the richness favored in materials for Grecian design. The combination of rosewood veneer, gilt carvings, marble top, silvered mirror and yellow silk upholstery create a dazzling effect. Although obscured by a second generation of acquisitions and the textural complication of wallpaper and bric-a-brac, the 1880s photograph gives a sense of the colorful environment that originally provided a foil for the commode (Fig. 12). Yellow silk imported from France covered the walls and this was elaborated into a magnificent "French" drapery made for the adjacent window by the Boston upholsterers Lawson & Harrington in 1835.[34]

The preservation of the cabinetmaker's copy of *The Modern Style*, artifacts, receipts and vintage photographs of the original locations provides an unusually clear picture of how an important commission was brought to completion thanks to King's book. British historians have generally considered Thomas King's contributions of limited value because they have associated him with middle-class production. If this view is consistent with his reception in Britain during his lifetime, it is important to note that *The Modern Style* held sufficient authority to be perceived as "high culture" by clients of wealth in the United States.

AMERICAN MIDDLE-CLASS RESPECTABILITY

Thomas King's influence in the United States extended beyond the creation of expensive furniture for wealthy patrons. Through the unac-

[34]Receipt from Lawson & Harrington, Upholsterers, Boston, 1835, in the George Peabody Papers, Peabody Essex Museum.

knowledged dissemination of images, his designs also infused American middle-class taste in less overt ways. In 1844, Thomas Webster and Mrs. Parkes published *An Encyclopædia of Domestic Economy* in London.[35] This 1225-page book began with a capsule history of architecture, proceeded through "Cooking for the Economist and Invalid" and ended with "Domestic Medicine." The *Encyclopædia* was popular in the United States and went through numerous American editions from 1845 to 1859. A third of its nearly "one thousand engravings" illustrate advice on what furniture was appropriate for the household and where each object belonged. The images ranged in complexity and expense from a utilitarian trestle table to "a sideboard of a more considerable size . . . made for large rooms, as they thus admit of great variety of ornament. . . ." A wood engraving of an elaborate sideboard shows a composite of elements dissected from Thomas King's "sideboard tables" (Fig. 13). The cabriole legs enshrouded with acanthus remind one of King's statement, "carving is required only in the boldest scrolls, or in the massive foliage. . . ." In Webster and Parkes's concoction, the legs and the cellarette are taken from Plate 55 and the concave plinth and some motifs for the backboard are variations on Plate 54. The central crest is a graceless rendering of King's intertwined palmettes and the Greek key motifs add a trite note.

[35]First published in London in 1844 as *An Encyclopædia of Domestic Economy* (London: Longman, Brown, Green, and Longman), 1844, 1847, 1852, 1861.
American editions of the same title were published by Harper & Brothers in 1845, 1847, 1848 and 1849. A later American version was titled *The American Family Encyclopedia of Useful Knowledge or book of 7223 receipts and facts.* It was distributed yearly by various publishers in New York between 1854 and 1859. Insight into its readership is revealed in: Minor Meyers, Jr., "Who Bought Webster and Parkes' *Encyclopædia of Domestic Economy?,*" *The Magazine Antiques*, Vol. CXV, No. 5, May 1979, pp. 1028–1031.

13. *Thomas Webster and Mrs. Parkes, sideboard, Figure 243,* An Encyclopædia of Domestic Economy *(1844). (This derives from King's Plates 54 and 55.) (University of Notre Dame.)*

14. *John Hall, two designs for wardrobes, Plate 37,* The Cabinet Maker's Assistant *(1840). (University of Notre Dame.)*

An Encyclopædia of Domestic Economy was not a book employed in the cabinet shop. Instead, it served to mold the middle-class imagination of how the ideal house should be managed—much the same role popular magazines play today. The book's extended popularity derived from "receipts," home remedies and advice for managing the household.

The final printing of *The Modern Style* occurred in 1862: the fact that examples of classical design first published in 1829 remained in circulation until the 1860s is odd, and it is curious to speculate whether this late edition was intended for the trade or the public. In either case the crude wood engravings in Webster and Parkes were concurrently available with the King originals from which they derive.

The rapid changes in fashion that occurred during the 1840s and '50s were not accounted for in the Webster and Parkes format but were promoted in books that challenged the classical modes in architecture and interior decoration.[36] Despite pervasive changes seen even in Thomas King's later titles, the Grecian images of *The Modern Style* remained "current" for a surprisingly long period.

The final example of *The Modern Style*'s influence in the United States involves the words of King's "Address" rather than its image bank. Sometime before 1835, an English artisan named John Hall immigrated to Baltimore.[37] In 1840, he published three books: one on houses, one on stair design and a third on furniture, *The Cabinet Maker's Assistant,* the first furniture-pattern book printed in the United States.[38] Although his bold geometries and heavy scrolls have suffered well-intentioned misnomers such as "Pillar and Scroll," like King and many early nineteenth-century contemporaries, Hall called his furniture "Grecian" and further distinguished it as "the present plain style of work" (Fig. 14).[39] These abstract variations on classical themes are becoming recognized as the culminating expression of a half-century of exploration of archaeological form in the domestic environment. The undeniable popularity of this furniture in the mid-nineteenth century reflects the spread of culture in an increasingly self-confident and democratic society.

[36]Andrew Jackson Downing, *The Architecture of Country Houses* (New York: D. Appleton & Company), 1850. Reprint (New York: Dover Publications, Inc.), 1969. "Interior Finishing of Country Houses" (pp. 364–405) and "Furniture" (pp. 406–460).

[37]Robert C. Smith, "John Hall, A Busy Man in Baltimore," *The Magazine Antiques,* Vol. XCII, No. 3, September 1967, pp. 360–366.

[38]Because of the book's historical importance, and despite extreme dissatisfaction with the designs it contained, *The Cabinet Maker's Assistant* was reprinted by Carl Dreppard in 1944. All three Hall titles are being reprinted with a new introduction in Thomas Gordon Smith, *John Hall and the Grecian Domestic Environment* (New York: Acanthus Press), 1995.

[39]Celia Jackson Otto, "Pillar and Scroll: Greek Revival Furniture of the 1830s," *The Magazine Antiques,* Vol. XXXI, No. 5, May 1962, pp. 504–507; John Hall, *The Cabinet Maker's Assistant* (Baltimore: John Hall), 1840, caption for Plate XII, Figures 64–68, p. 25.

John Hall was not an innovator. His chronicle of massive forms and abstract curves reflects an American approach to Grecian design that was apparent as early as 1833 in the well-known broadside of Joseph Meeks & Sons.[40] At the same date King's book was inspiring elaborate furniture for George Peabody, the planar aspect of the Grecian mode was already established. Although the wardrobe and wing dresser of Hall's Figure 175 on Plate 37 is similar to wardrobes shown on King's Plates 61 and 83, precise links such as we have seen earlier cannot be made. The most tangible connection between the books is clear only after comparing the introductory texts; King's "Address" and Hall's "Preface."[41]

[40]Robert C. Smith, "Late Classical Furniture in the United States, 1820-1850," *The Magazine Antiques*, Vol. LXXIV, No. 6, December 1958, pp. 519–523; Marshall B. Davidson and Elizabeth Stillinger, *The American Wing at the Metropolitan Museum of Art* (New York: Alfred A. Knopf), 1985, p. 164. Roughly half of the images depict the abstract contours of the "John Hall type" whereas the other half imitate images from a book published 1826–28 by one of King's older contemporaries, George Smith: *The Cabinet Maker and Upholsterer's Guide.*

[41]In reproducing the "Address" and "Preface" side by side, the words actually copied by Hall are emphasized in bold and those paraphrased are in italics.

It is apparent that Hall both plagiarized and paraphrased King's text when writing his introduction. After recognizing this, it is interesting to sort out the differences between the texts. For Hall, objects of emulation came from Europe, not specifically Paris. This may indicate Hall's awareness of the variations made on Empire types by French Restauration and Germanic Biedermeier designs. On the other hand, the statement may simply be a gratuitous reassurance for American readers who needed a European imprimatur.[42] Because the "labor-saving" features of the broad scrolls were as important to Hall as the economy involved in "composition ornament" was to King, one component of Hall's intended audience was the cabinetmaker. Nevertheless, Hall departed from King when he also dedicated his book to "persons who may order furniture" so that it could be "executed without any misunderstanding." These were the American clients who also read Webster and Parkes.

[42]Charles Lane Venable, *Philadelphia Biedermeier: Germanic Craftsmen and Designs in Philadelphia, 1820–1850* (Ann Arbor, MI: University Microfilms International), 1986.

Thomas King, *The Modern Style of Cabinet Work Exemplified*	John Hall, *The Cabinet Maker's Assistant*
Address	**Preface**
Novelty and **Practicability** constitute the **present Designs;** and the **economical arrangement** of Material will, it is presumed, **render the** *Work of peculiar service* **to the Cabinet** *Manufacturer.* **Originality** *generally pervades;* **a few** *specimens only of Work already* **executed** are introduced, which, **being** of a description **highly approved,** are inserted under the idea of perfecting the collection. **As far as possible,** the English **style is** carefully **blended** *with Parisian* **taste:** *and a chaste contour* and **simplicity of parts** is attempted **in all the objects** which, being confined in dimensions and form, present some difficulty in the adaptation of Grecian, Roman, and Gothic Ornaments. Considering the clearness with which the Plates have been executed, it is expected that directions in the working parts would be useless, especially as the wood made use of, and the retaining all the ornament, must be optional, or regulated according to the richness required; but it may be remarked, that many of the plain parts of breadth were intended for rich veneer, finely polished, and that in the gilded parts, carving is required only in the boldest scrolls, or in the massive foliage; while composition ornament mostly may be used for rosettes, enriched mouldings, ornamental borders, and generally in the minute detail.	**Novelty,** simplicity and **practicability** are blended with the **present designs,** in which **originality** *mostly prevails,* **a few** of those *designs have been taken from works previously* **executed,** in consequence of their **being highly approved. As far as possible,** the **style** of the United States **is blended** *with European* **taste,** *and a graceful outline* and **simplicity of parts** are depicted **in all the objects.** The present work will not only be *useful to the* **manufacturer,** but of great importance to persons who may order furniture, as they will be enabled to select their patterns and have them executed without any misunderstanding. The great variety of scrolls shown in this work, with instructions for drawing them, will afford great facilities to the artizan in applying them to a great variety of work not enumerated in the present collection. The short treatise on perspective will be found of the utmost importance to every cabinet maker, as they can acquire, by a very little study of those principles, a sufficient knowledge to enable them to draw with accuracy any piece of work that may present itself to their mind. Throughout the whole of the designs in this work, particular attention has been bestowed in an **economical arrangement** to save labor; which being an important point, is presumed *will* **render the** *collection exceedingly useful* to **the cabinet**-*maker.*

It is clear that *The Modern Style of Cabinet Work Exemplified* influenced furniture design in the United States during the mid-nineteenth century. Renewed access to King's designs should "render the Work of peculiar service" to the current generation of cabinetmakers (Fig. 15). Combined with many other impulses in contemporary society, this reprint could well contribute to the revival of classical forms and principles in our built environment.

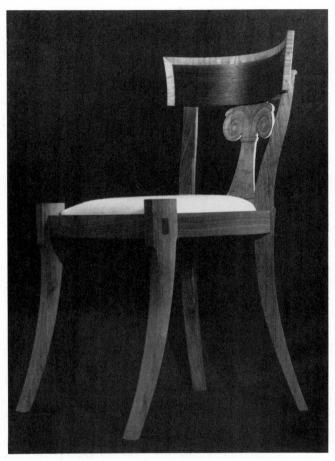

15. *Robert Brandt, archaic Grecian chair (1993). (University of Notre Dame.)*

APPENDIX I

BIBLIOGRAPHY OF REFERENCES
TO THOMAS KING

John Andrews, *Victorian and Edwardian Furniture* (Woodbridge, England: Antique Collector's Club), 1992, pp. 173, 186, 210, 213–214, 251, 296.

Anonymous, Review of "A Compilation of Splendid Ornamental Designs," *The Albion* (London: Wm. Boucher), June 7, 1834.

Elizabeth Aslin, *Nineteenth Century English Furniture* (New York: Thomas Yoseloff), 1962, p. 27.

Geoffrey W. Beard and Christopher Gilbert, *Dictionary of English Furniture Makers 1660–1840* (London: W. S. Maney and Son, Ltd.), 1986, p. 515.

Geoffrey W. Beard, *The National Trust Book of English Furniture* (New York: Viking Penguin), 1985, pp. 48, 54, 72, 202–203.

Frances Collard, *Regency Furniture* (Woodbridge, England: Antique Collector's Club), 1987, pp. 28, 126–127, 152–157, 161–162, 231, 274.

John Saville Crofton, *The London Upholsterer's Companion* (London: John Williams), 1836. A critique of *The Upholsterers' Accelerator* appears on pp. x–xi.

Peter Floud, "Furniture," *The Connoisseur Period Guides: The Early Victorian Period, 1830–1860* (New York: Reynal & Company), 1958, pp. 37, 39, 45, 48.

Wendell Garrett, *Neo-Classicism in America, Inspiration and Innovation, 1810–1840* (New York: Hirschl & Adler Galleries, Inc.), 1991, p. 78.

John Gloag and Clive Edwards, *A Complete Dictionary of Furniture* (Woodstock, NY: The Overlook Press), 1991, p. 375.

John Gloag, *The Englishman's Chair* (London: George Allen & Unwin Ltd.), 1964, pp. 210–213, 229–232.

John Gloag, *Guide to Furniture Styles: English and French, 1450–1850* (London: Adam and Charles Black), 1972, pp. 7, 220, 221, 228.

Simon Jervis, *Dictionary of Design and Designers* (New York: Facts on File), 1984, pp. 270–271.

Edward T. Joy, *The Country Life Book of Chairs* (London: Country Life Ltd.), 1967, pp. 76–79.

Edward T. Joy, *English Furniture 1800–1851* (London: Sotheby Parke Bernet), 1977, pp. 118–119, 147–151, 227, 256.

Edward T. Joy, "The Overseas Trade in English Furniture in the Nineteenth Century," *Furniture History* (London: The Furniture Historical Society), 1970, pp. 69, 72.

Edward T. Joy, *Pictorial Dictionary of British 19th Century Furniture Design* (Woodbridge, England: Antique Collector's Club), 1986, pp. xxii–xxiii and throughout.

John Claudis Loudon, *The Architectural Magazine and Journal of Improvement in Architecture, Building and Furnishing and the Various Arts and Trades Connected Therewith* (London: Longman, Orme, Brown, Green & Longman).
Notices and reviews of books by Thomas King:
• May 1834, Art. VI, p. 137: *A Compilation of Splendid and Ornamental Designs from Foreign Works.*
• December 1834, Art. II, p. 370: *Working Ornaments and Forms; Full Size.*
• July 1835, Art. VII, p. 304: *The Cabinet Maker's Sketch Book of Plain and Useful Designs.*
• November 1835, Art. IX, pp. 512–513: *The Cabinet Maker's Sketch Book of Plain and Useful Designs (Chair and Sofa Work).*
• August 1837, Art. IV, pp. 394–399: *The Cabinet Maker's Sketch Book of Plain and Useful Designs, Vol. II, consisting of Cabinet Work Generally.*

Florence M. Montgomery, *Textiles in America, 1650–1870* (New York: W. W. Norton & Co.), 1984, pp. 72, 73, 409.

Barbara Morris, "Textiles," *The Connoisseur Period Guides, The Early Victorian Period 1830–1860* (New York: Reynal & Company), 1958, pp. 115, 117–119, Plate 69.

John Morley, *Regency Design 1790–1840* (New York: Harry N. Abrams), 1993, pp. 408–409.

Claudio Paolini, *Il Bello "Ritrovato"* (Novara: Istituto Geografico DeAgostini), 1990, pp. 283, 298 (note 17), 567 (note 8).

E. W. Symonds & B. B. Whineray, *Victorian Furniture* (London: Country Life Ltd.), 1962, pp. 99, 175.

Page Talbott, "Seating Furniture in Boston, 1810–1835," *The Magazine Antiques*, Vol. CXXXIX, No. 5, May 1991, pp. 956–969.

Berry B. Tracy, *19th Century American Furniture and Other Decorative Arts* (New York: New York Graphic Society), 1970. Selected bibliography of 18th and 19th century sources—furniture, no page.

Clare Vincent, "John Henry Belter's Patent Parlour Furniture," *Furniture History* (London: The Furniture History Society), 1967, p. 99.

Gail Caskey Winkler, "Introduction," *An Analysis of Drapery* [1819] and *The Upholsterer's Accelerator* [1833], (New York: Acanthus Press), 1993, pp. v–xxvi.

APPENDIX II

LIST OF TITLES BY THOMAS KING

I would like to acknowledge the generosity of many libraries in Britain, Canada and the United States which have allowed me to consult their holdings in compiling this list. The National Art Library at the Victoria and Albert Museum, The Department of Prints and Illustrated Books at The Metropolitan Museum of Art, the collection of John Bedford and The Grand Rapids Public Library in Grand Rapids, Michigan, have been particularly valuable resources.

*copies known to exist

*1. Cabinet Maker's Sketch Book of Plain and Useful Designs (Cabinet Work)	1835
*2. Cabinet Maker's Sketch Book of Plain and Useful Designs (Chair and Sofa Work)	1836
3. Compilation of Splendid and Ornamental Designs from Foreign Works	±1833
*4. Decorations for Windows & Beds	1827–28
*5. Designs for Carving & Gilding	1829; 1836
*6. Fashionable Bedsteads with Hangings	1839–42
*7. Fashionable Window Cornices and Hangings with Glass Frames &c.	1839–42
8. Fashionable Upholstery Work	<1835
9. French Designs for Ornamental Drapery of Windows and Beds	<1835
*10. Household Furniture, Comprising 38 Designs of Utility and Elegance	1823–24
*11. Illustrations of Fashionable Cabinet Furniture	<1834
12. Modern Designs for Drapery and Valances Displayed in Beds and Windows	<1835
*13. Modern Designs for Household Furniture	1827–28
*14. Modern Style of Cabinet Work Exemplified	1829; 1832; 1862
*15. New and Elegant Designs for Chairs	±1825
*16. Original Designs for Cabinet Furniture	±1836
*17. Original Designs for Chairs and Sofas	±1836
*18. Shop Fronts and Exterior Doors	<1834
*19. Specimens of Furniture in the Elizabethan & Louis Quatorze Styles	>1842
*20. Specimens of the Present Style of Drapery Connected with Upholstery Furniture	<1834
*21. Supplementary Plates to The Modern Style of Cabinet Work Exemplified	<1835
*22. Upholsterers' Accelerator	1833
*23. Upholsterer's Guide: Rules for Cutting and Forming Draperies [contents same as Upholsterers' Accelerator]	1848
24. Upholsterer's Pocket Collection of Fashionable Designs	1835

THE MODERN STYLE

OF

CABINET WORK

Exemplified,

IN NEW DESIGNS, PRACTICALLY ARRANGED ON 72 PLATES,

CONTAINING 227 DESIGNS, (INCLUDING FRAGMENTAL PARTS.)

London:

PUBLISHED BY T. KING, 17, GATE STREET, LINCOLN'S INN FIELDS.

Price £1 12s.

[TITLE PAGE OF THE FIRST EDITION (1829).]

ADDRESS.

―――――

NOVELTY and Practicability constitute the present Designs; and the economical arrangement of Material will, it is presumed, render the Work of peculiar service to the Cabinet Manufacturer. Originality generally pervades; a few specimens only of Work already executed are introduced, which, being of a description highly approved, are inserted under the idea of perfecting the collection. As far as possible, the English style is carefully blended with Parisian taste: and a chaste contour and simplicity of parts is attempted in all the objects which, being confined in dimensions and form, present some difficulty in the adaption of Grecian, Roman, and Gothic Ornaments. Considering the clearness with which the Plates have been executed, it is expected that directions in the working parts would be useless, especially as the wood made use of, and the retaining all the ornament, must be optional, or regulated according to the richness required; but it may be remarked, that many of the plain parts of breadth were intended for rich veneer, finely polished, and that in the gilded parts, carving is required only in the boldest scrolls, or in the massive foliage; while composition ornament mostly may be used for rosettes, enriched mouldings, ornamental borders, and generally in the minute detail.

18, WILMOT STREET,
BRUNSWICK SQUARE, LONDON.

[REPRODUCED FROM THE FIRST EDITION (1829).]

DESCRIPTIVE LIST OF THE PLATES.

PLATE

1.—PIER SLABS, for Carving—composition Ornament—and Gilding; the second is adapted for a glass beneath it, if thought proper.

2.—PIER SLABS. The lower one is supported by brackets only.

3 & 4.—SCROWL SUPPORTS, designed for gilding, and intended for Slabs, in the piers or the end of a Drawing-room. In attempting the greatest variety they are shewn upon paws, stump feet, blocks, plinths, &c.

5.—FIRE SCREENS. In the mount of the third a chaste effect is produced by silk cord and small tassels, (which must be flat next the screen,) and suspended from rosettes. This is adapted particularly for a rich taboret.

6.—FIRE SCREENS. The stand of the third is intended to have fine wood in the plain part, and French polished. The cross fluting of silk is formed from a breadth of silk each way, drawn narrower in the centre by being held with four studs.

7.—A SLIDING SCREEN.

8.—SCREENS. The first in the old French style; a slide may rise from either, if required.

9.—SOFAS. The principal ornamental parts are intended to be carved in relief only, and the leaves in the front rail are first ploughed like a moulding and then cut into form.

10.—SOFAS. The carved work of these should be of very delicate projection, or a vulgarity in the appearance would otherwise be the consequence.

11.—COUCHES. The very plain parts, which frequently occur in the turned work, (and here are seen in the legs of the first Couch) are intended to shew the beauty of the French polish; and when a hanging husk appears as from the scrowl, it should be in slight relief only.

12.—COUCHES. The rosettes introduced here and in many of the other plates, it will be remembered, are intended to be turned by the lathe into the form, and then channeled into leaves, being a considerable saving in the expence of carving.

13 & 14.—DESIGNS FOR SOFAS AND COUCHES. Placing, at one view, a very great variety of the different forms in use.

15 & 16.—PARLOUR CHAIRS. Massive and plain, as the purpose requires; in the first a half null moulding sunk is introduced in the top and in the front rail.

17.—DRAWING ROOM CHAIRS. The first, second, and third, shew various shapes for stuffed backs; the fourth is adapted for fine veneer, especially the splat, which will require a rich curl.

18.—DRAWING ROOM CHAIRS. The legs of the first have not so much work as at a glance appears, as the form and projection of the leaves is the work of the lathe, and afterwards they are channelled into leaves. The small knobs on the upper parts of the legs in the second chair are turned separately, and fixed on after the other parts are finished.

19.—DRAWING-ROOM CHAIR BACKS. The three upper ones are adapted for stuffed backs; the first and third being specimens in the old French style.

20.—BED ROOM CHAIRS.

21.—BED ROOM CHAIRS. The first and second are intended to be stained, and the third and fourth for japanned work.

22.—HALL CHAIRS. The second is left plain in the back for the crest to be painted.

23.—HALL SEATS.

24.—EASY CHAIRS. The panel in the side of the first is formed of silk lace, the colour of the material with which the chair is covered.

25.—EASY CHAIRS, WITH INCLINED SEATS. In the first the eliptic side-rail is designed to disguise the descent of the seat towards the back, which is rather objectionable in its appearance.

The second is of more simple construction; and (the same as the first) the back keeps the form of the person.

26.—EASY CHAIRS.

27.—READING OR LOUNGING CHAIRS, with the backs sufficiently low to serve as rests for the arms.

28.—EASY CHAIRS, WITH INCLINED SEATS. In the second design the back may be lowered by removing the stud (which goes through the brass plates projecting at the back), and placing it in a lower hole, thereby suiting the inclination of the back to the fancy. This is a very useful pattern, and extremely simple.

29.—EASY CHAIRS. The seat of each is stuffed upon a moving frame, which slides forward, and gives the back (being hinged to the frame-work of the seat) any inclination required.

30.—MUSIC CHAIRS, varying particularly in the form of the backs.

31.—MUSIC STOOLS, the stands of which are of turned work, ornamented with channelled leaves.

32.—FOOTSTOOLS, contrasting the several shapes in use.

33.—A CABINET, of fanciful richness, intended for the reception of curiosities: the lower shelves for large specimens, and the upper part for smaller objects. Looking-glass might here be introduced at the back, which, besides being highly ornamental, would throw a light around the choice articles upon the shelves: to be formed of rosewood, with shelves covered by a material of the colour best calculated to display the curiosities to advantage.

34.—PIER TABLES. The columns of the first are plain to display the beauty of the French polish.

The Pilasters and Pillars of the second are fluted in the upper part, and reeded below, thereby producing a great richness of effect.

35.—PIER TABLES. In the second design the pillars may be veneered, with the caps and bases slipped on; glass is intended to be at the back of each.

36.—A COMMODE AND GLASS, for the end of a Drawing-room, with the doors decorated the same as described for the screen in the foregoing Plate.

37.—A COMMODE AND GLASS, for the end of a Drawing Room. On the doors is plaited silk, in the form of pipes, which are strained behind the fringe down to the style, thereby keeping them in their places.

38.—COMMODES. In the second is introduced a very chaste pattern of brass-work for the doors; the intersections of the wires are rivetted by small studs, and may be with or without silk behind them.

39.—COMMODES. The fluted silk upon the doors of the lower design is terminated by fringe, which should be exceeding neat, and placed in its situation after the material is strained, and tack'd.

40.—COMMODES.—In the first the ornamental corners in the uppermost parts of the doors are intended to be merely a perforated thin piece of the wood, with a turned and channelled rosette laid on; the silk with which the doors are fluted may be seen through the open ornament, or a back ground of the wood used.

41.—LOO TABLES. The first has a very plain turned pillar. It may here be observed, that whenever the work of the lathe is of this description, additional care should be bestowed in having the contour as correct as possible, its shape being its only beauty. The second has a column glued up hollow, veneered, and with carved ornaments laid on.

42.—LOO TABLES.

43.—CARD TABLES.

44.—CARD TABLES. The support of the first is mostly the work of the lathe, which, if well polished, would have a beautiful effect. The pillar of the second has leaves which are chiefly formed with the other turned work, and then channelled into leaves. This is a very useful ornament, and frequently occurs. The block is a pattern very prevalent in France.

45.—STANDS FOR LOO TABLES, shewing a variety of shapes in the pillars and blocks.

46.—STANDS AND PILLARS FOR CARD TABLES.

47.—OCCASIONAL TABLES.

48.—OCCASIONAL TABLES.

49.—DESIGNS FOR OCCASIONAL TABLES. The third in the old French style; the fourth has the support in the hexagon form.

50.—A SIDEBOARD.

51.—A SIDEBOARD.

52.—SIDEBOARDS, very plain. The truss supports of the second may be veneered in front, and French polished.

53.—SIDEBOARDS of a plain description.

54.—A SIDEBOARD TABLE, with looking-glass at the back. The massive supports in front may be veneered in the middle, and French polished.

55.—A SIDEBOARD TABLE, with the front legs placed cornerways, as in the old style.

56 & 57.—SIDEBOARD BACKS. The plain panels in the centre were intended for very fine wood.

58.—SUPPORTS FOR SIDEBOARD TABLES. The plain parts were intended to be highly polished; the fifth is in the old French style.

59.—MOVING SIDEBOARDS.

60.—AN EXTENDING DINING TABLE, upon a very approved principle.

61.—A WARDROBE. At each end a door opens the depth of the piece of furniture, with shallow shelves for shoes, &c.

62 & 63.—LEGS FOR TABLES; amongst which are specimens of square, partly square, reeded, plain turned, carved, and other patterns.

64.—A GOTHIC BOOKCASE. Generally gothic work is considered extremely expensive in execution; however, this design is arranged with the expectation of its being manufactured at a moderate price.

65.—A BOOKCASE.

66.—A BOOKCASE. The panels on the lower doors are formed by a fillet laid on, and the corners (of turned work) are made flush with the surface of the fillet.

67.—A BOOKCASE, with a secretaire drawer.

68.—A DWARF BOOKCASE. Between the columns is looking glass, which will give a lightness and brilliancy to the piece of furniture which it would not otherwise possess; and to prevent waste of room, small doors may open at the ends for books, the depth which the two pillars occupy.

69.—A DWARF BOOKCASE, with a secretaire drawer, and doors at the ends (top and bottom) to lock up books; the depth of the recesses would, of course, be the same as the width of the double column in front.

70.—GENTLEMEN'S SECRETAIRES, shewing two designs; the desk part is fixed to the flap, and of course lets down with it.

71.—AN EXTENDING DINING TABLE, upon a plan of great strength.

72.—BOOKCASE DOORS.

73.—BOOKCASE DOORS. The third shews a gothic pattern, and it may be observed in the sixth that the glass joining behind the ornament, running up the centre and across, gives it the effect of one sheet of glass only.

74.—Pediments for Bookcases, &c. The wreath introduced in the first, is partly turned and afterwards finished with a little carving; it is useful in many instances, and generally has an excellent effect.

75.—Designs for Capitals, and shewing different patterns for the surfaces of the pilasters.

76 & 77.—Designs for the Fitting up of a Library, or for open (detached) Book-cases. The endeavour has been to shew a collection, varying from each other as much as possible; the sixth and seventh, as may be seen, are gothic patterns.

78.—Japanned Wash Stands. The first contains, at the bottom, a cupboard, and by its angular shape is adapted to stand in a corner.

The second has two supports only, in the French manner; the space below the basin is to hold the water-bottle and glasses.

79.—Wash Stands.

80.—Wash and Dress Stands. The glass is affixed to each, independent of the top, which rises against it when used for washing.

81.—Wash Stands.

82.—A Winged Bookcase. The broad pilasters are intended to be part of the doors, and of course open with them.

83.—A Wardrobe. The styles and panels of the outside door are flush, and the ornaments at the corners sunk.

84.—Tea Poys. Varying considerably from the others in the forms of the blocks; the supports of the lower two are of very plain turned work, intended for French polish.

85.—Tea Poys. The rounded front of the first was designed to display the beauty of fine veneer; the last is also calculated for the same effect. In this plate, and in others, throughout the work, the attempt has been to give the greatest possible variety of forms in the blocks.

86.—Ladies' Work Tables. The top of the first lifts up and shews a circle of divisions, containing pin-cushion, scissors, needle-cases, &c., the centre of which is open to the space below for fancy work.

The second has the top made to slide back, that the table may be opened without disturbing whatever might be upon it, and the interior is fitted up the same as the first, except the forms will be square instead of circular.

87.—Ladies' Work Tables. The first has a draw in front and a pouch formed by ribs of thick wire, which falls, and forms an opening, by disengaging the snap beneath the centre of the draw.

88.—Fancy Tables. The first with a top for Chess, and the third a specimen in the old French style.

8

89.—WRITING DESKS. A door opens in the side of the first, as shewn in the other. The second has a drawer in front, which, when opened, a flap lies upon the top (of any inclination required) for writing; pens, ink, wafers, &c. are in divisions at the sides.

90.—A GOTHIC WINGED BOOKCASE.

91.—LIBRARY TABLES, adapted for oak or other wood.

92.—A TOILET. It may be observed the glass rises or slides down the pilasters, as shewn in the profile, by the aid of weights and lines, so that when pushed quite down the lower edge will rest upon the plinth, and the ornamental top only be seen above; it is intended to stand against a window. The small draws on each side were designed as a great convenience to the person when sitting in front of the table, and the trays on the top intended for candles, &c.

93.—A TOILET. Stuffing is introduced upon the streacher rail, as a rest for the feet; and a draw is at each end instead of the usual one in front, as being more convenient for the person while sitting at the table.

94.—FOLIO STANDS. The upper part of the first is hinged at the angles, by which it occupies less room, without removing the folios. The second is of most simple construction, and shuts up like a butler's tray: the rest for the folios is swivel-hinged at one side, and rises when the other parts are closed together.

95.—MOVING BOOK SHELVES. The supports of the first are intended to be from inch mahogany, and very slightly carved; those of the second contrast with the former, by being without any carved work whatever.

96.—FLOWER STANDS. The first and second are mostly the work of the lathe, and in parts channelled into the form of leaves. The small scrolls in the upper part of the third, cause it to be there in a triangular shape, just beneath the top, which is round. The fourth is in the old French style.

97.—FRENCH BEDSTEADS. The first is formed in the Parisian manner, and the exceedingly plain surfaces are for the purpose of shewing to advantage fine veneer and the French polish; the head and foot outside take the form of the side quite across. The second, in the English style, has square pillars and pannels at the head and foot.

98.—FRENCH BEDSTEADS. The first has the columns round in the upper part (excepting the extreme top), and is intended to be highly polished. The lower design is particularly calculated for rich veneer.

99 & 100.—PILLARS FOR BEDSTEADS. The first and second are specimens of entirely turned work; the ninth is a square column, with panels of rich veneer, to be French polished; and the eighth and twelfth have round knobs in the upper part, which are to be turned separately and placed on when the rest is finished.

Pier Slabs.

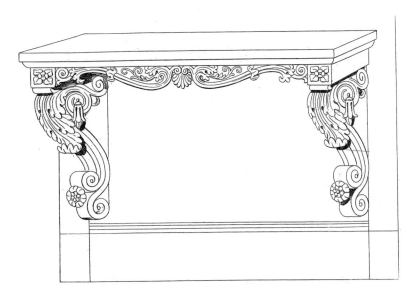

Pier Slabs.

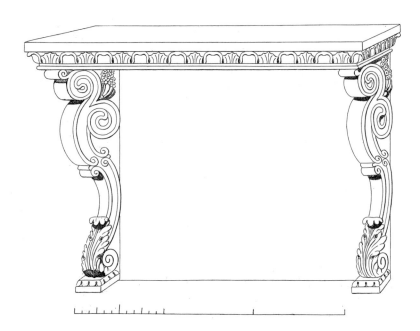

Screens.

Screens.

Fire Screens.

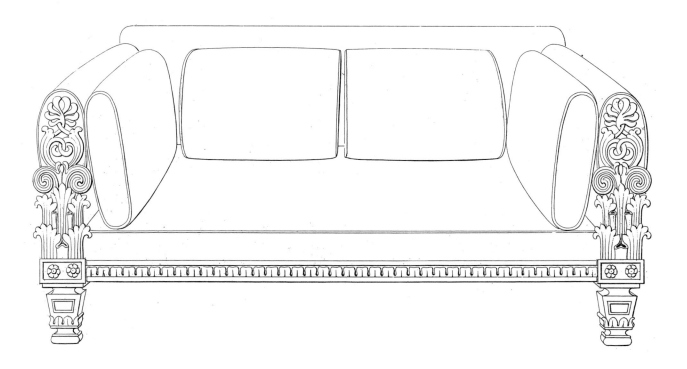

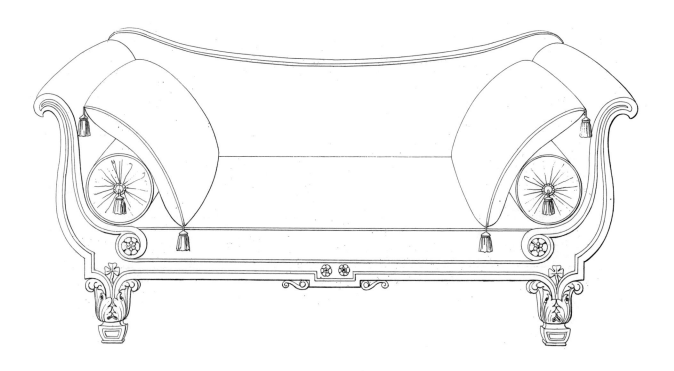

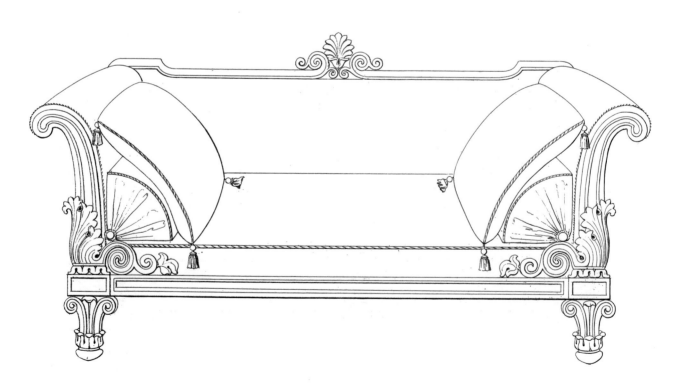

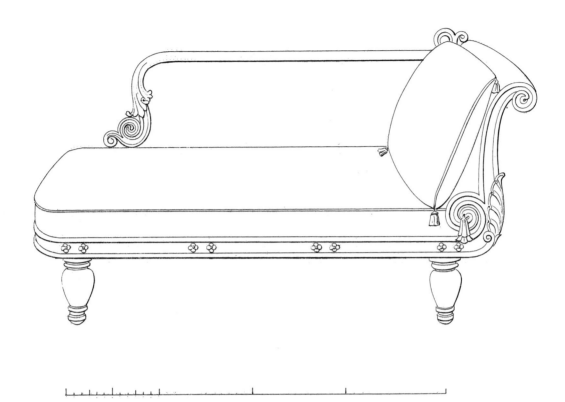

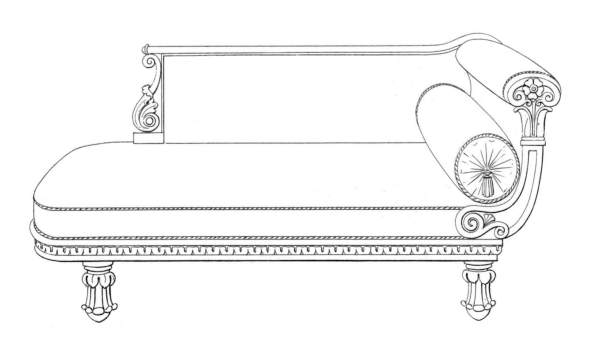

Sofa Ends.

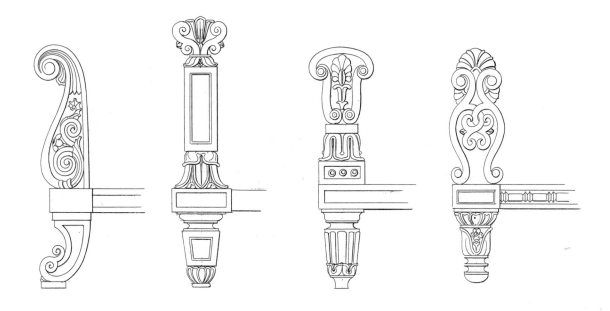

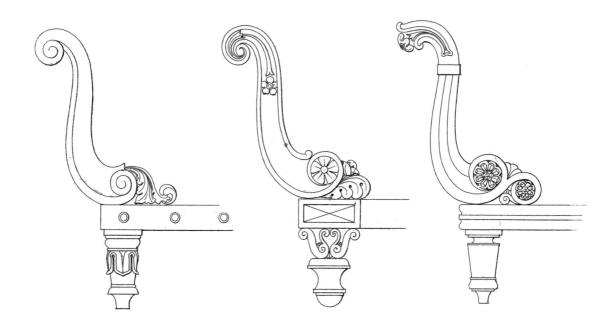

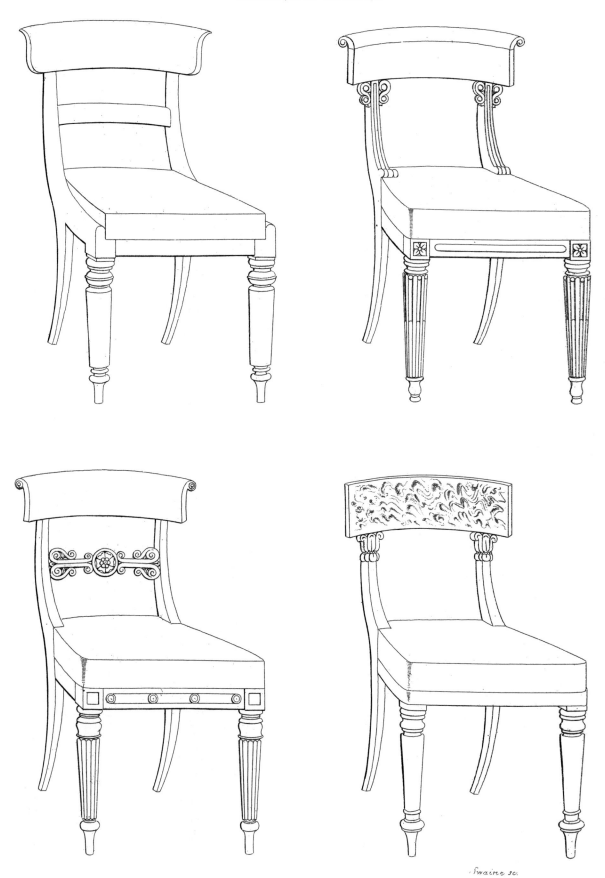

Swaine sc.

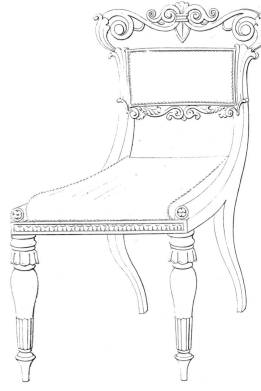

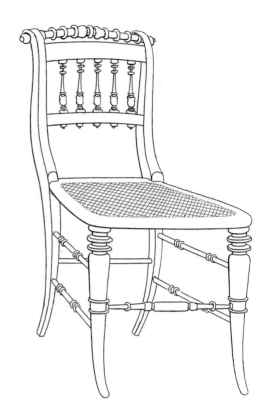

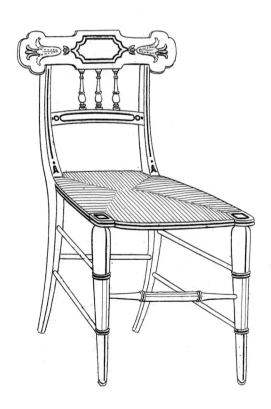

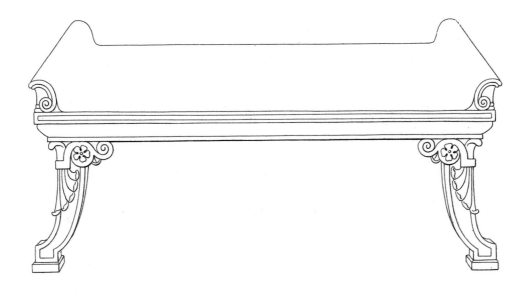

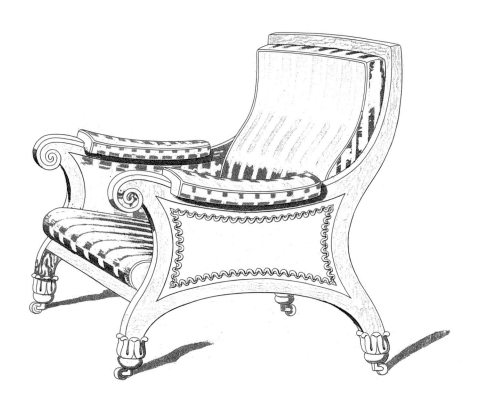

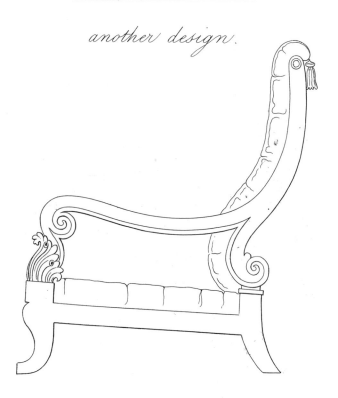

another design.

27

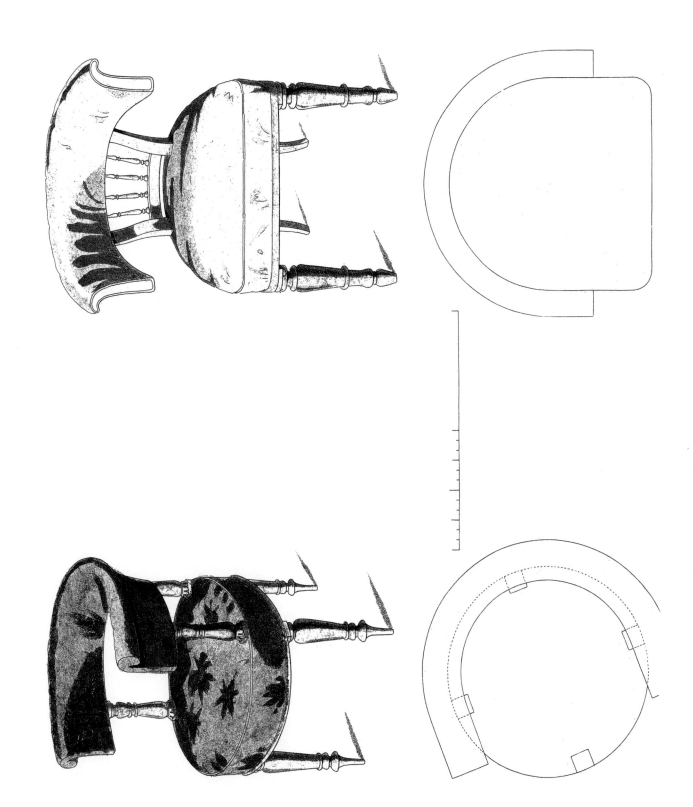

Reading or Lounging Chairs.

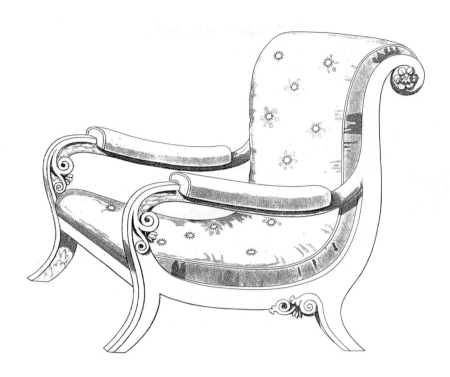

another design.

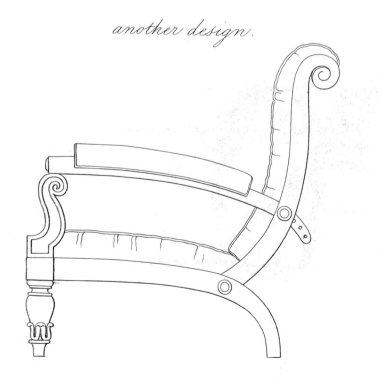

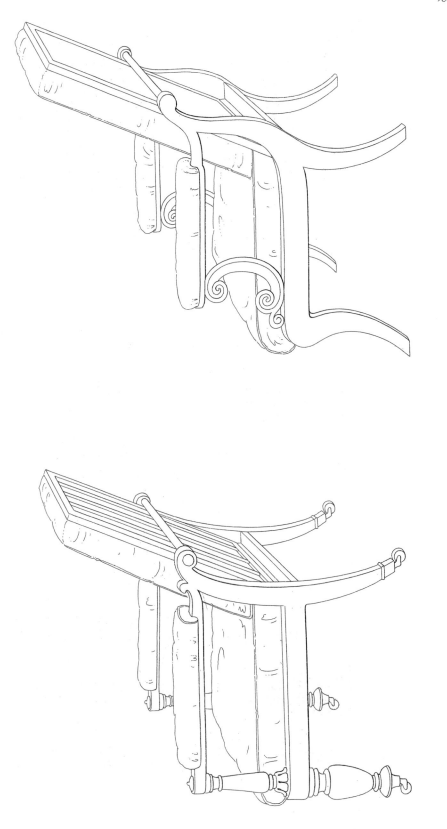

Chairs with inclining backs.

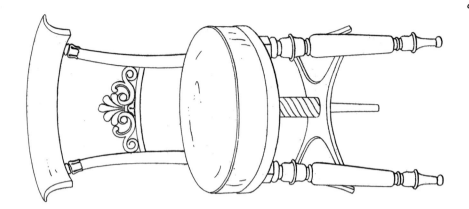

Music Chairs.

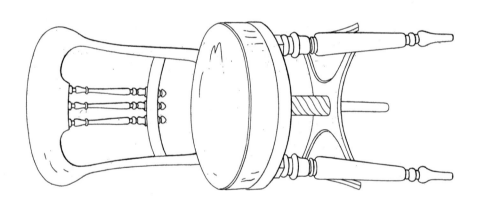

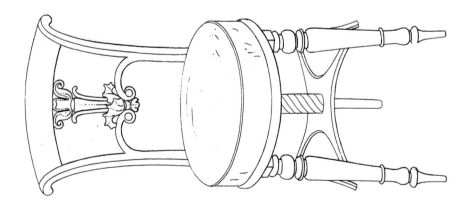

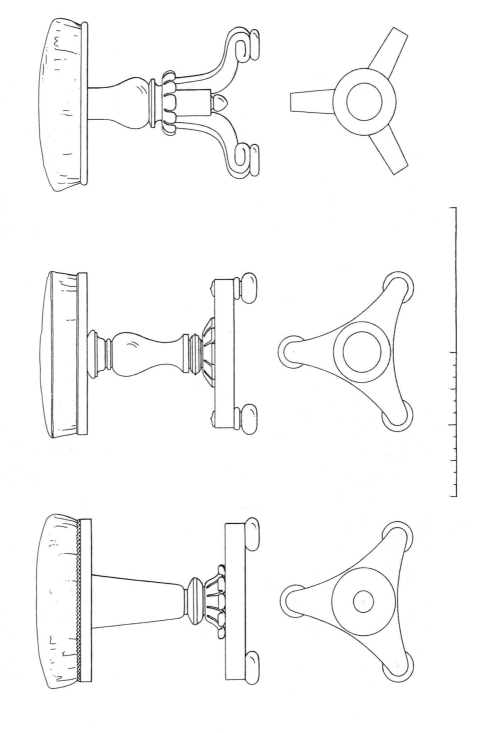

Music Stools.

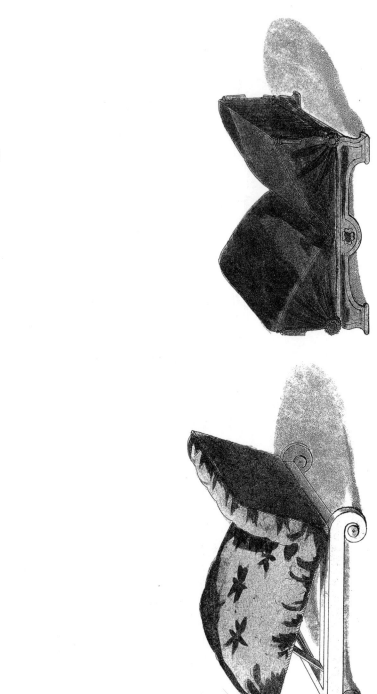

Footstools.

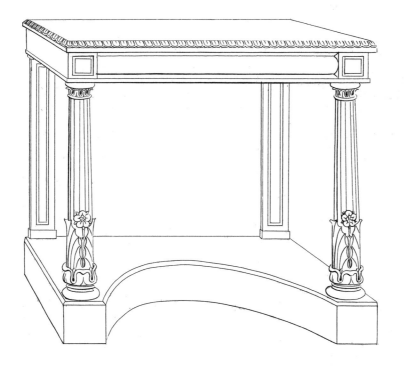

J. Henshall.

Commode and Glass

COMMODES.

¼ full Size.

¼ full size.

Swaine fc.

Plan of the plinth.

1/4 full size.

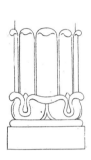

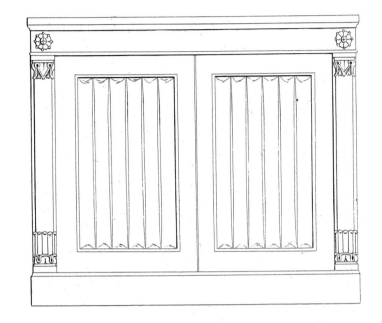

1/4 full size.

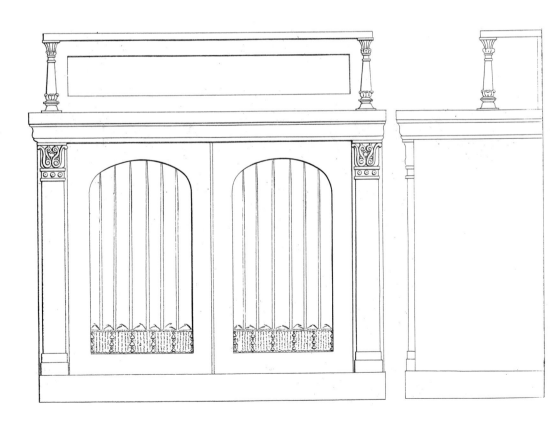

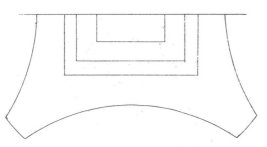

CIRCULAR LOO TABLES.

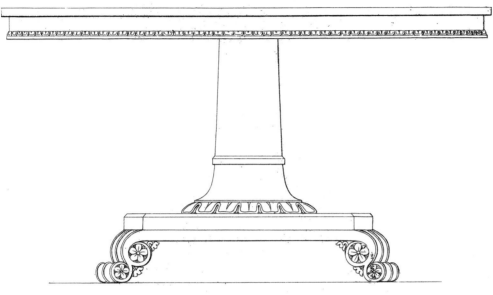

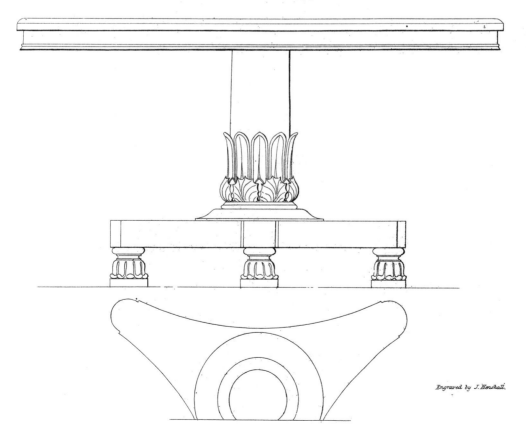

Engraved by J. Henshall.

CIRCULAR LOO TABLES.

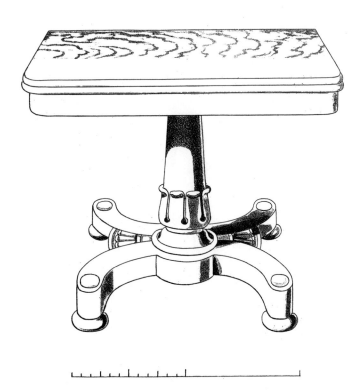

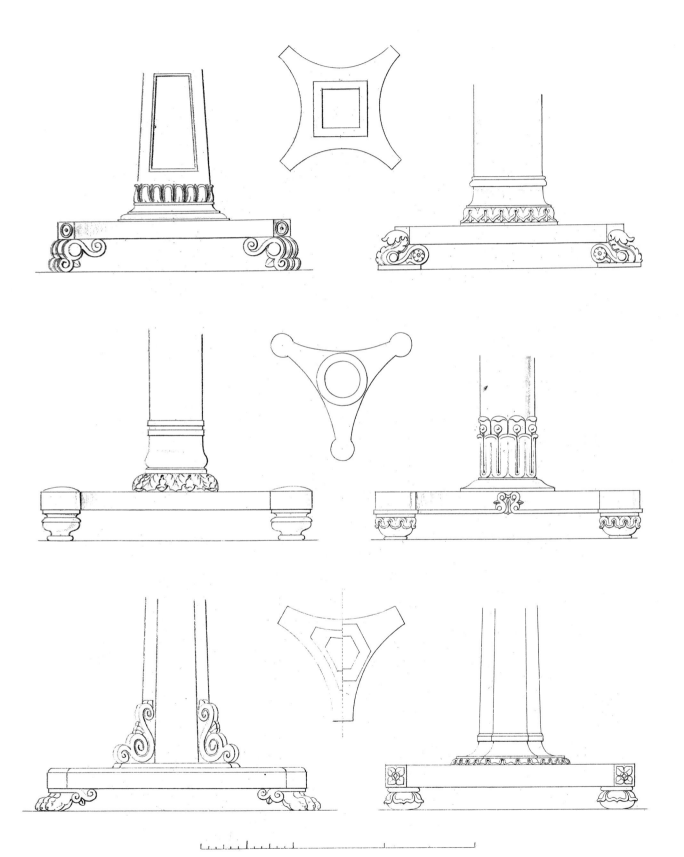

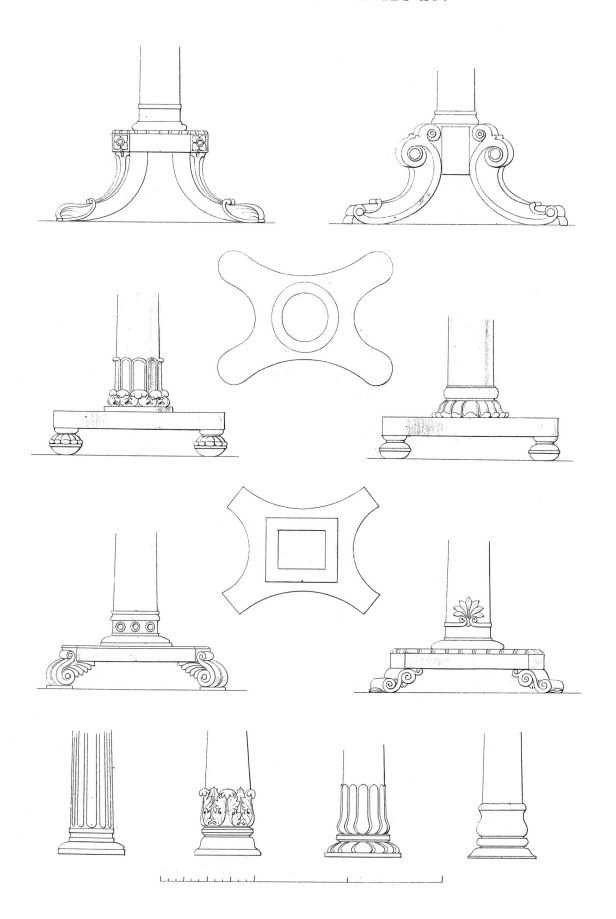

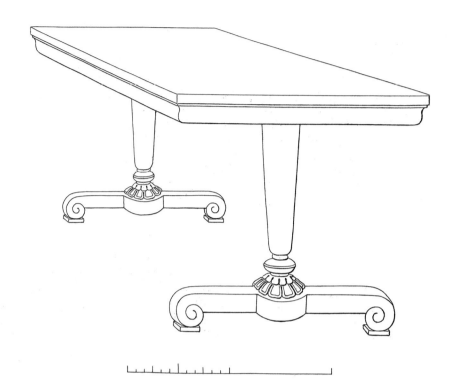

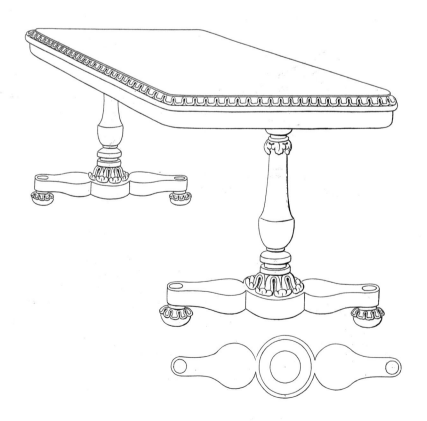

Occasional Tables.

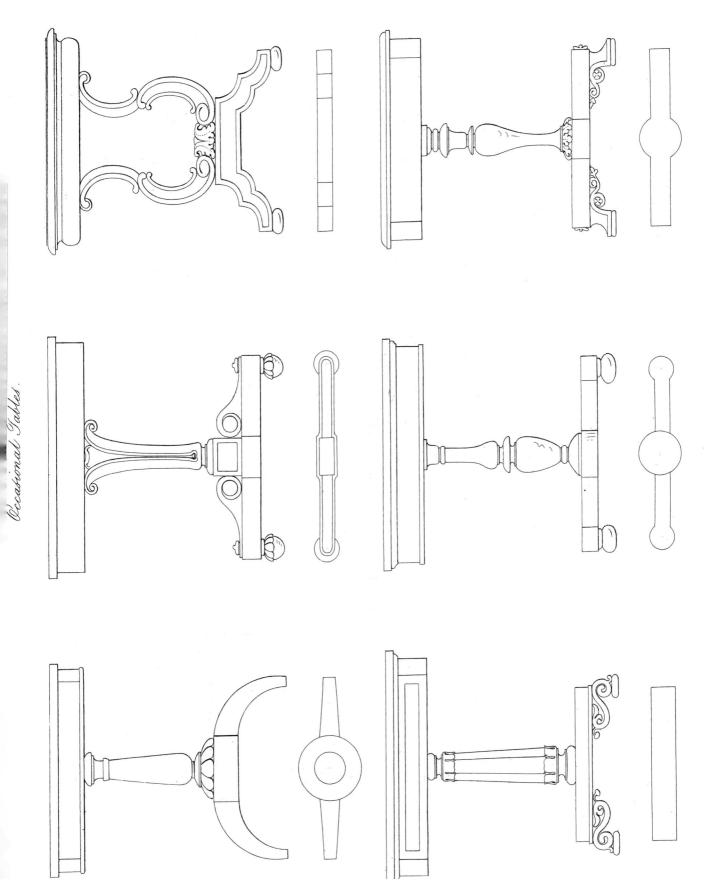

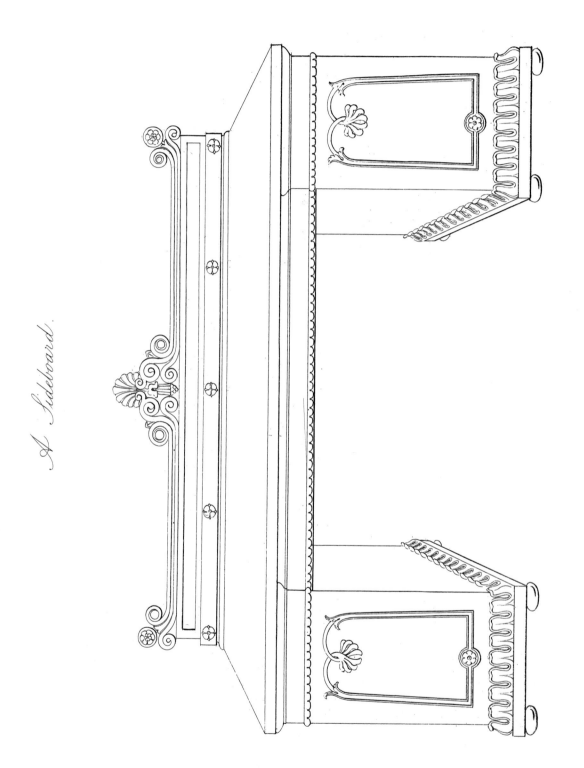

A Sideboard.

A Sideboard.

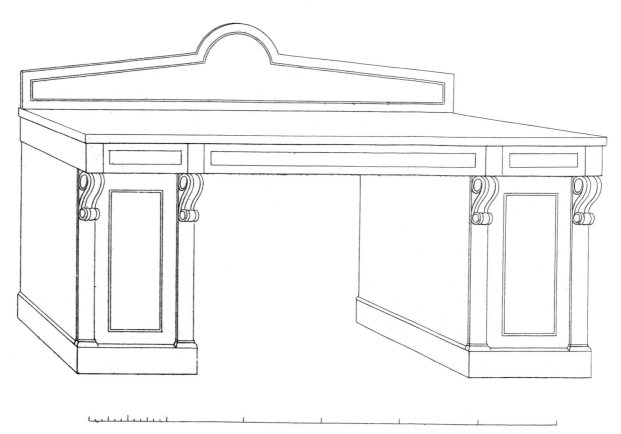

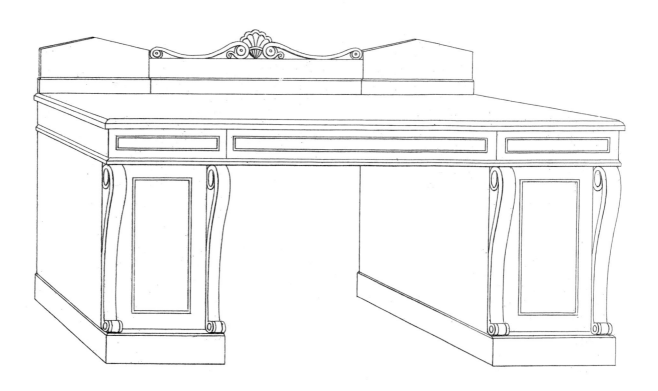

A Sideboard Table.

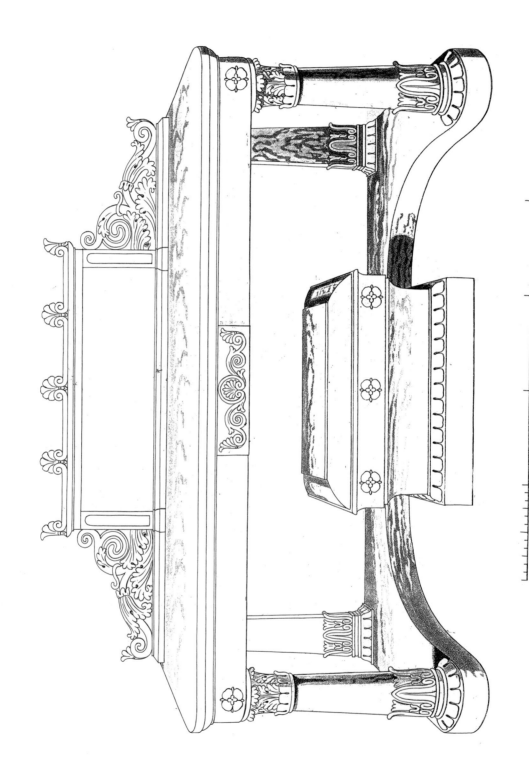

A Sideboard Table.

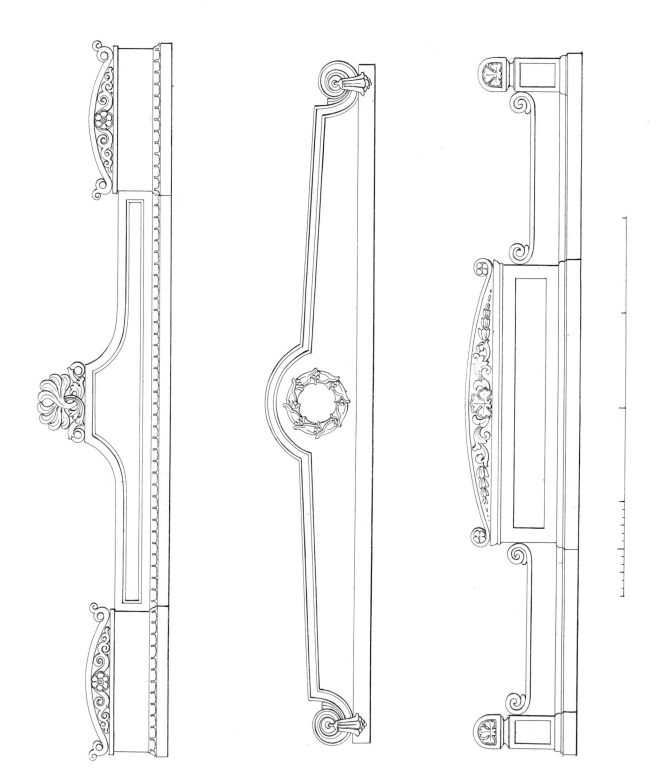

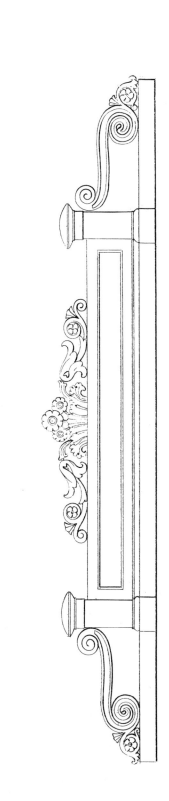
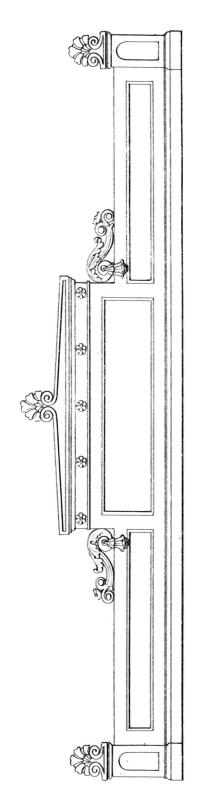

Sideboard Backs.

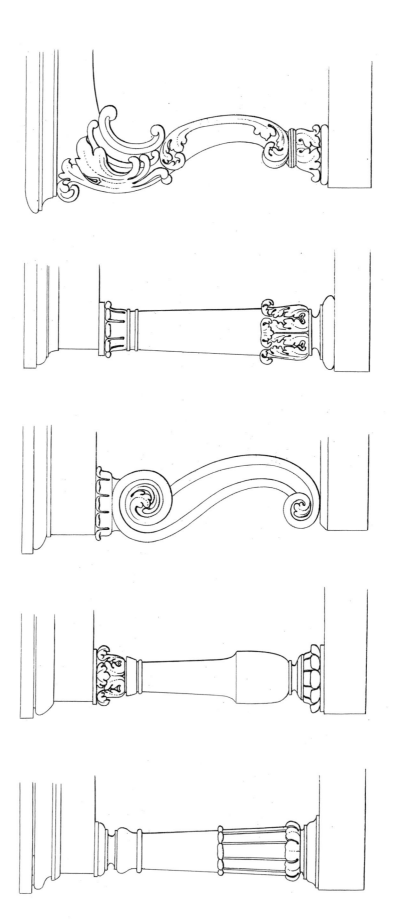

Supports for Sideboard Tables.

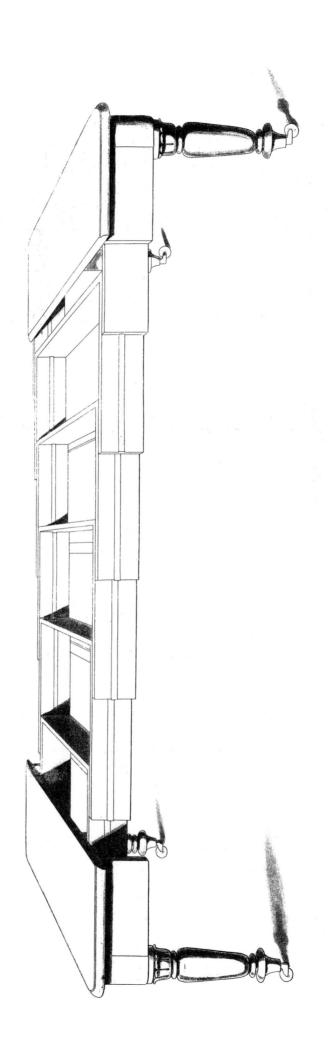

An extending Dining Table.

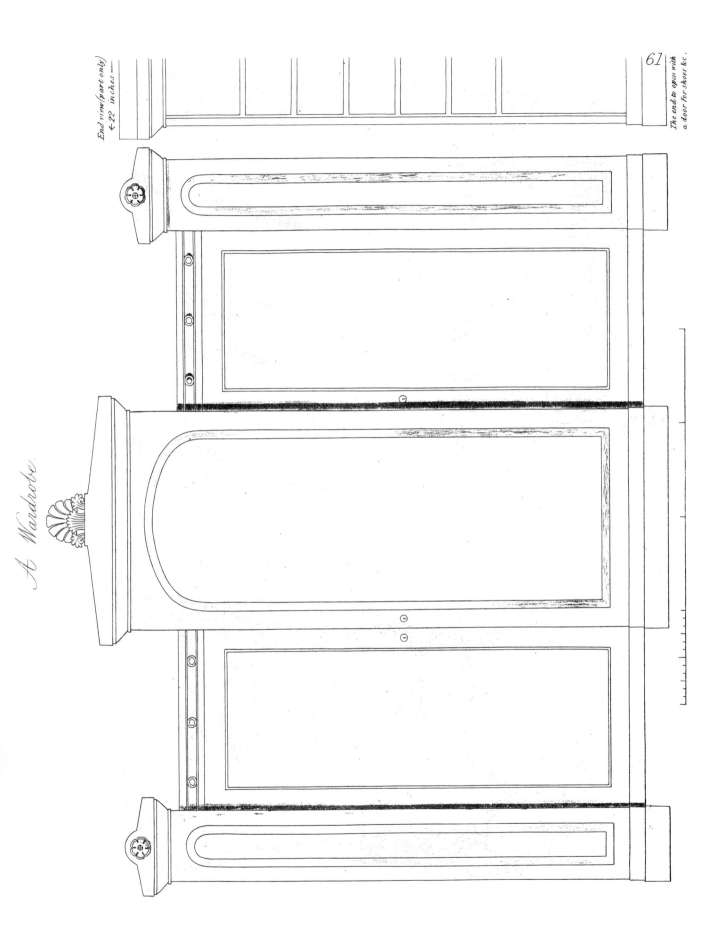

A Wardrobe.

End view (part only)
← 22 inches →

The end to open with
a door for shoes &c.

61

LEGS FOR TABLES.

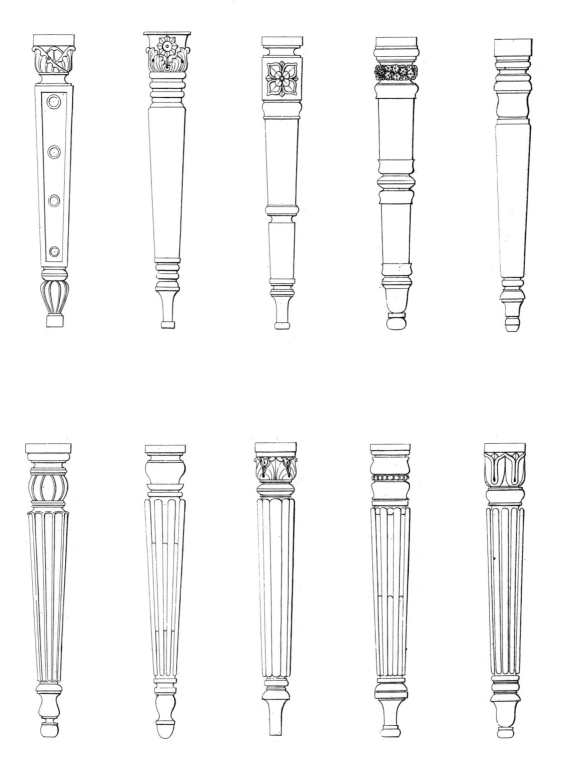

LEGS FOR TABLES.

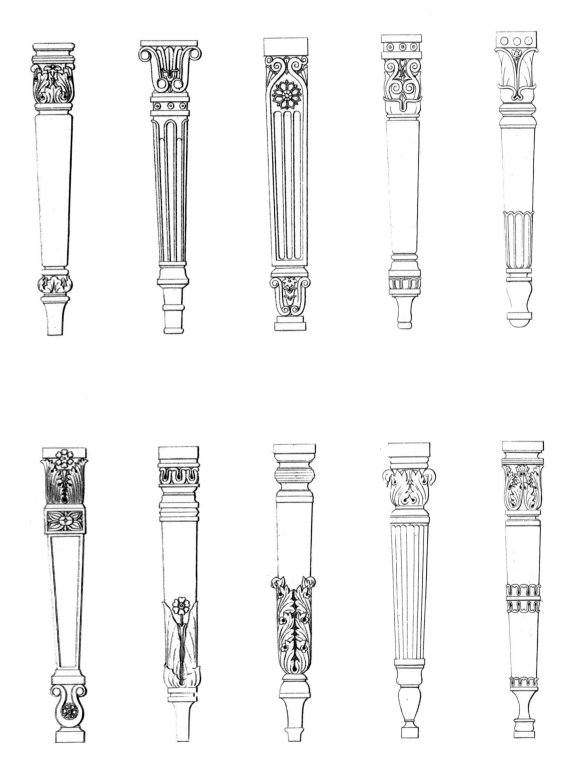

A Gothic Bookcase.

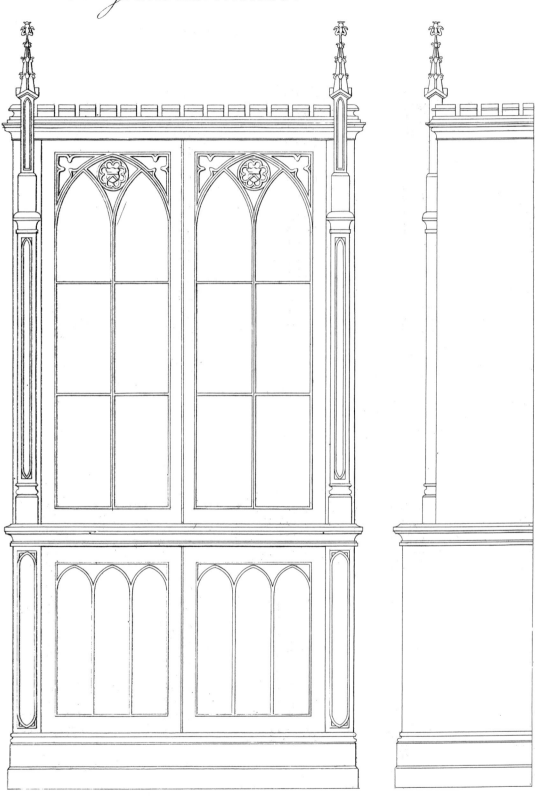

A Bookcase.

A Bookcase.

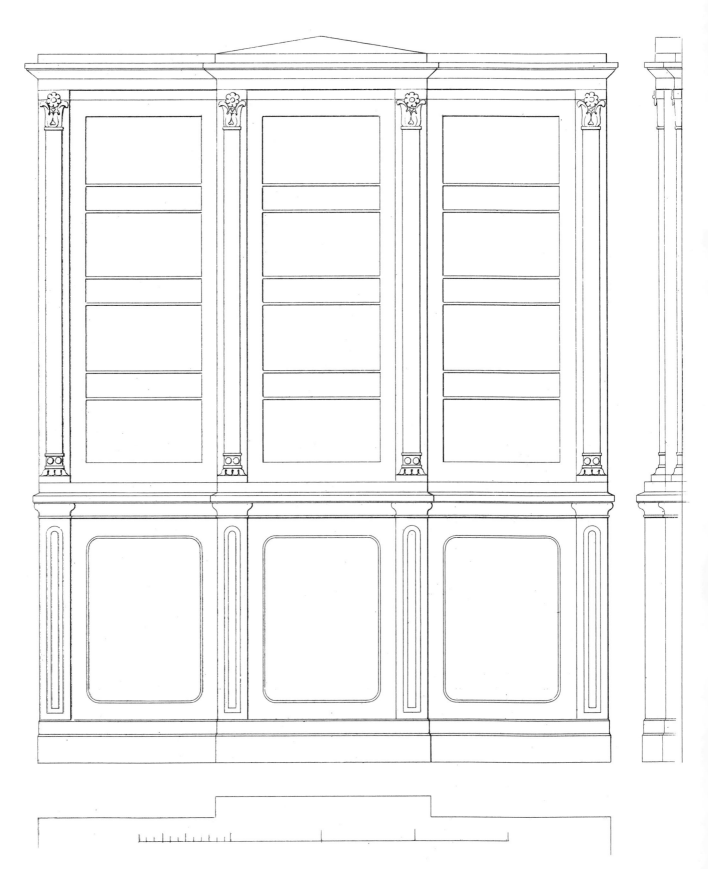

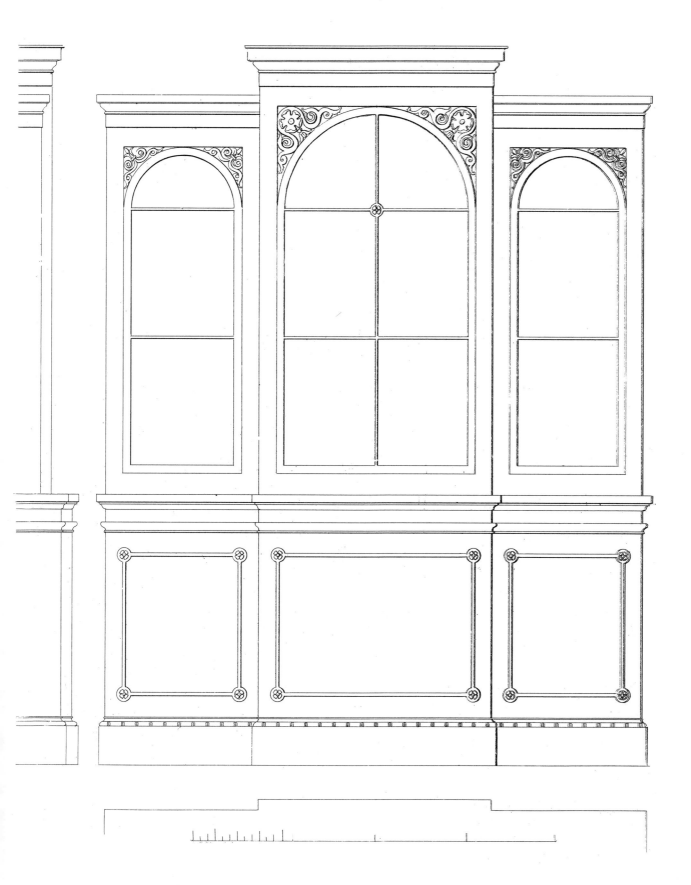

A Bookcase.

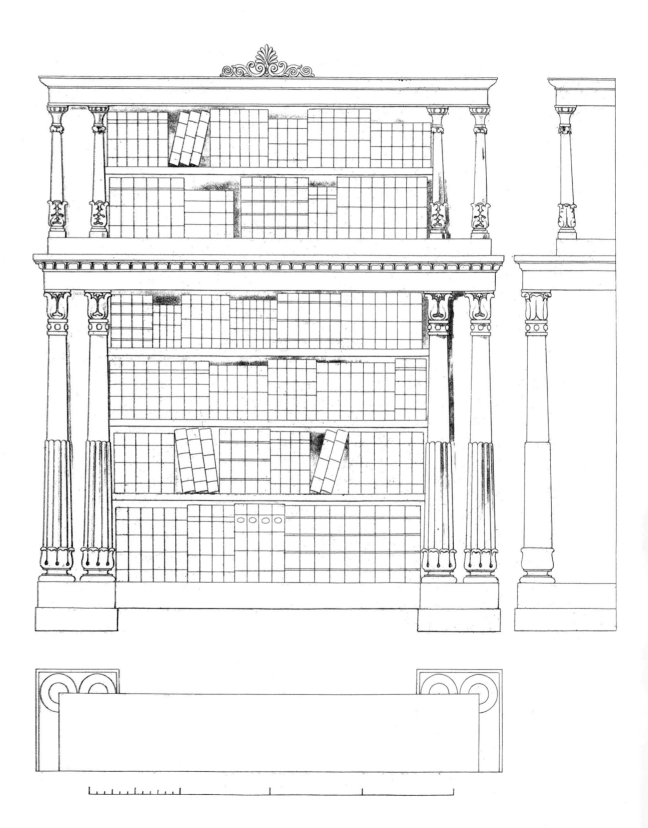

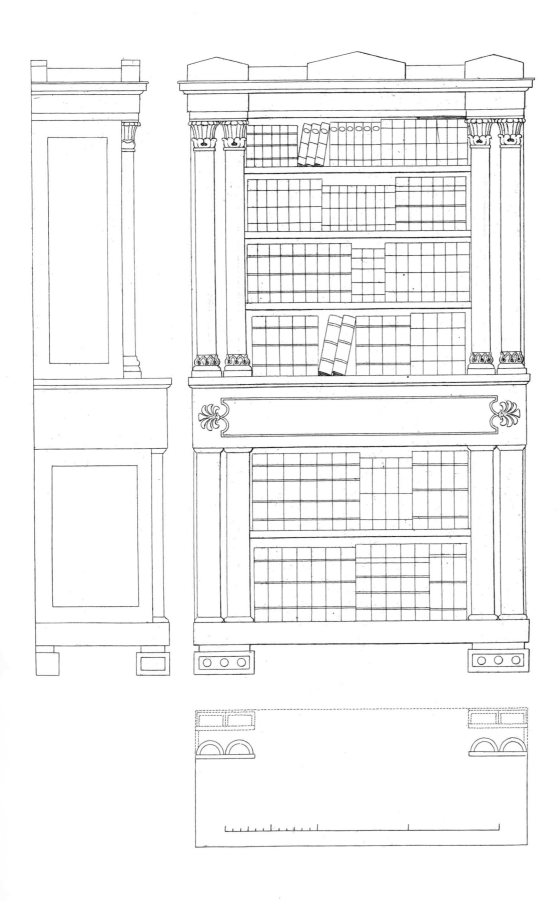

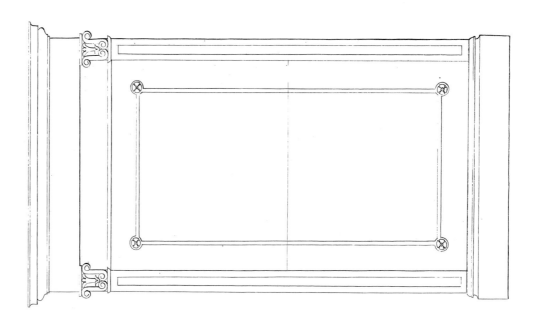

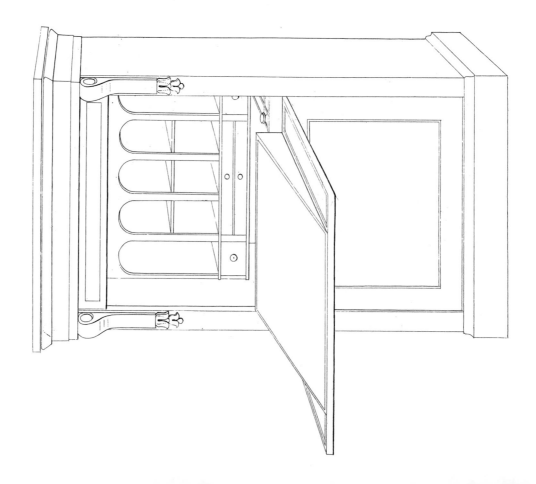

An extending Dining Table.

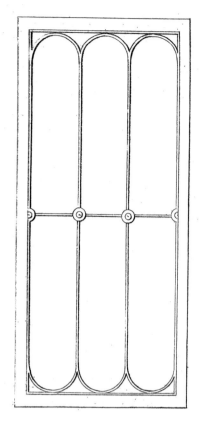
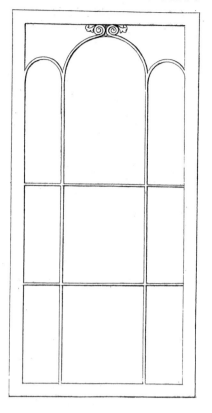
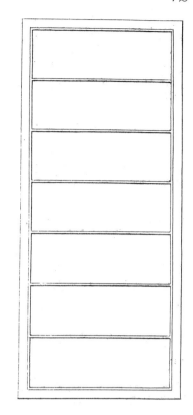
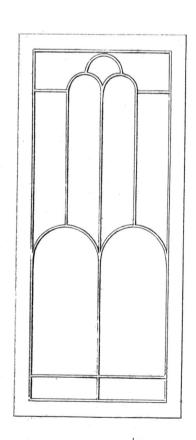

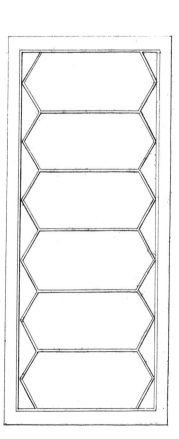

Engraved by J. Henshall.

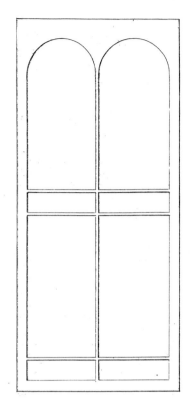

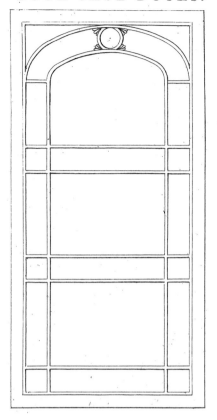

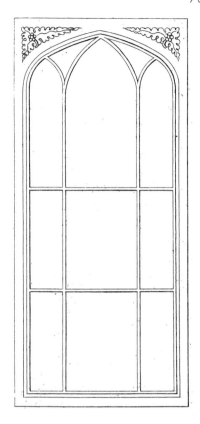

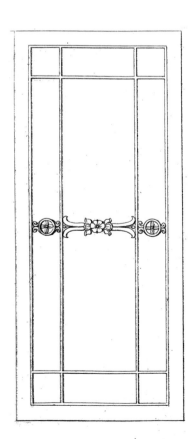

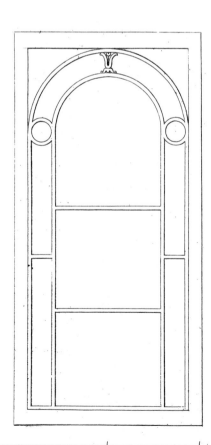

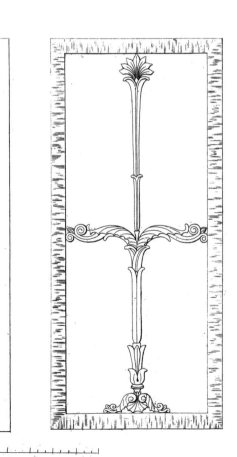

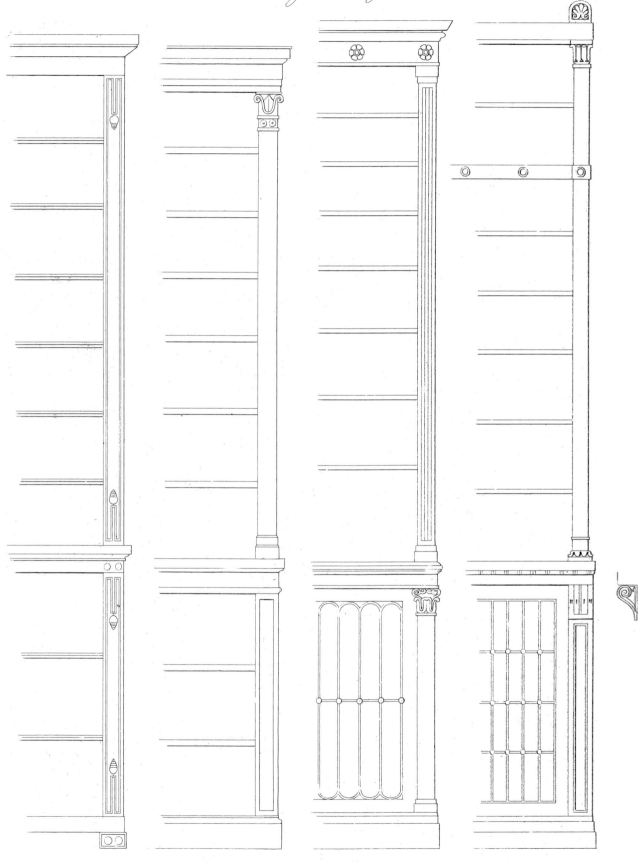

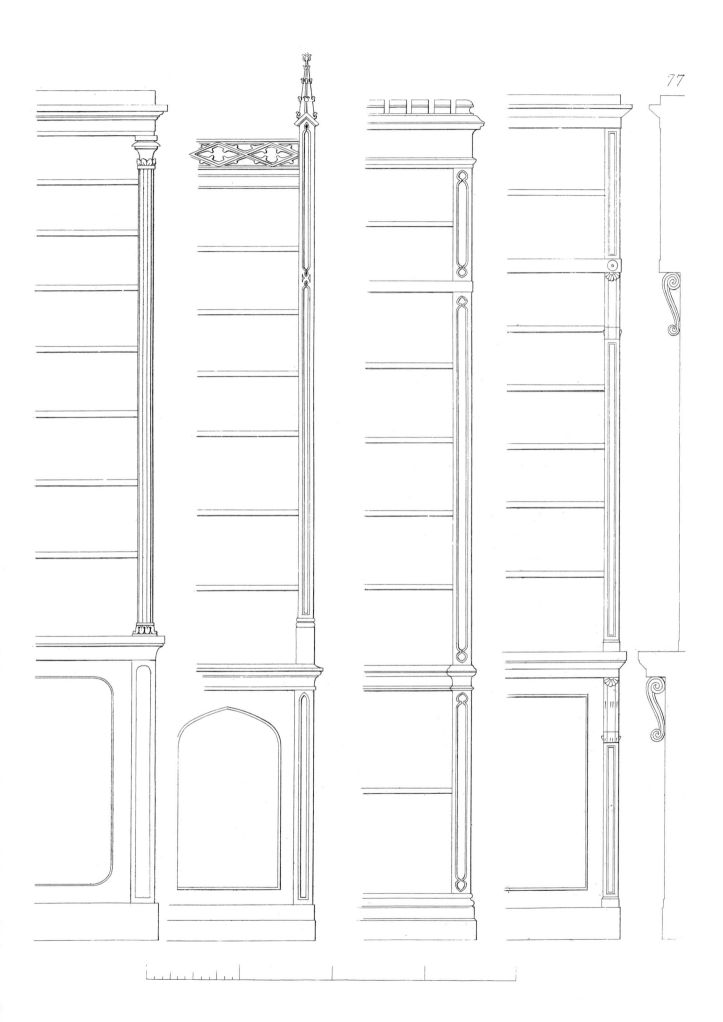

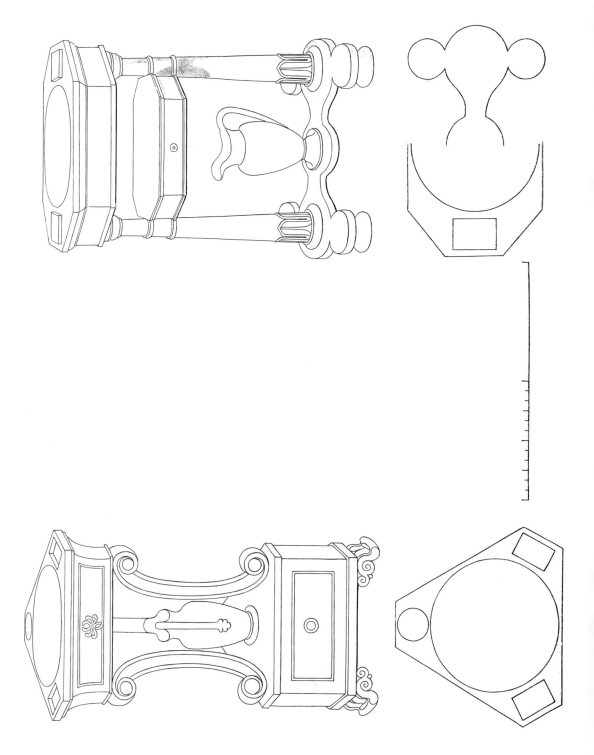

Wash Stands

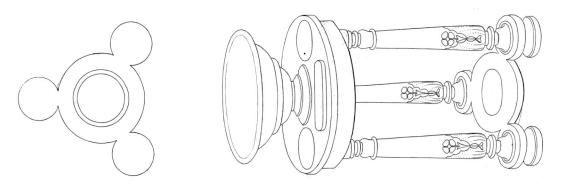

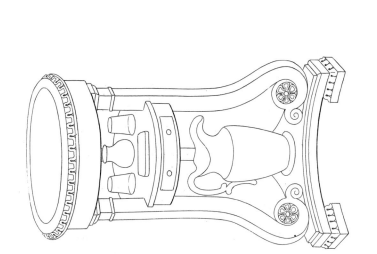

Wash Stands.

Wash & Dress Stands.

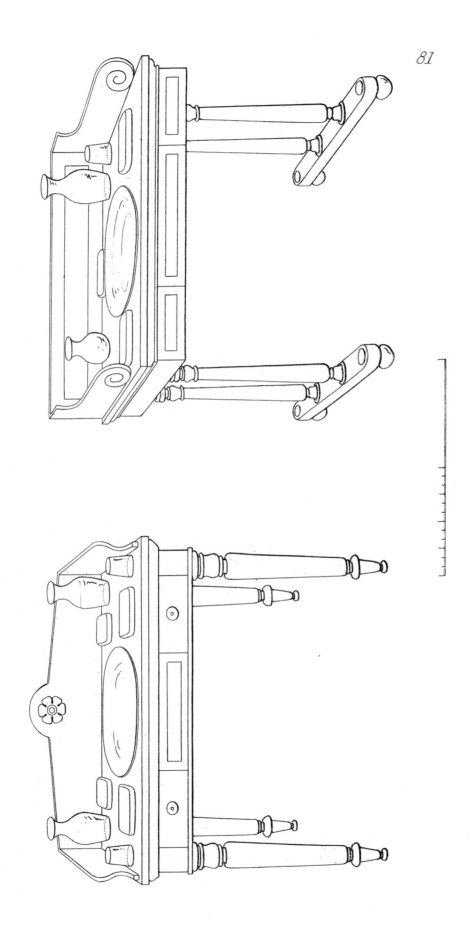

*81*

Wash Stands.

A Winged Bookcase.

83

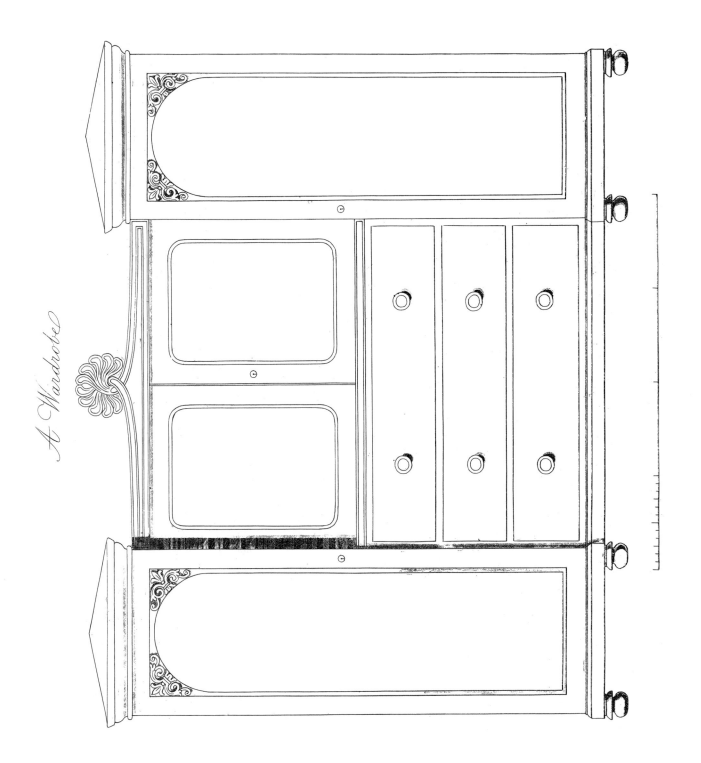

A Wardrobe

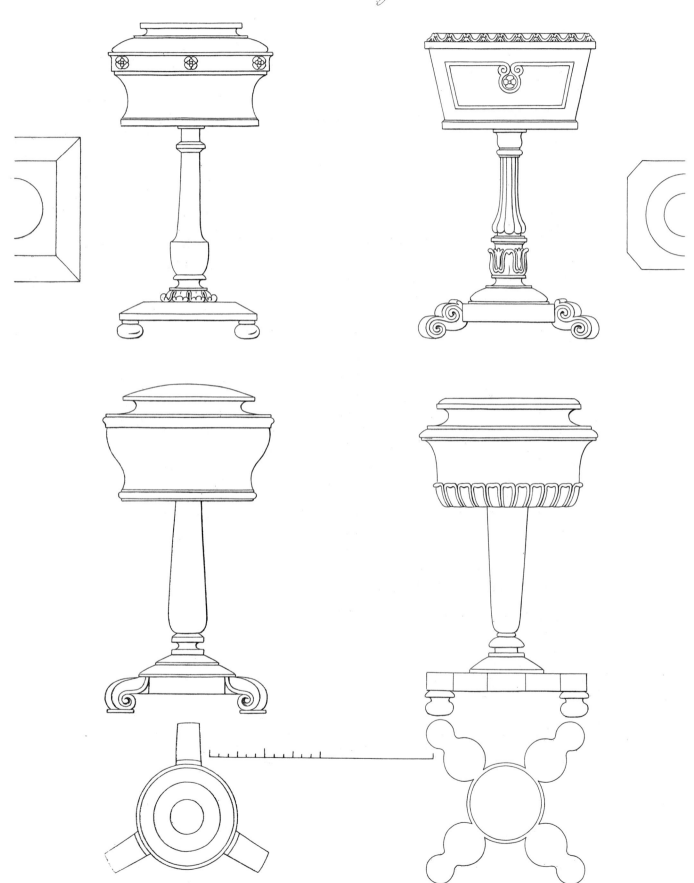

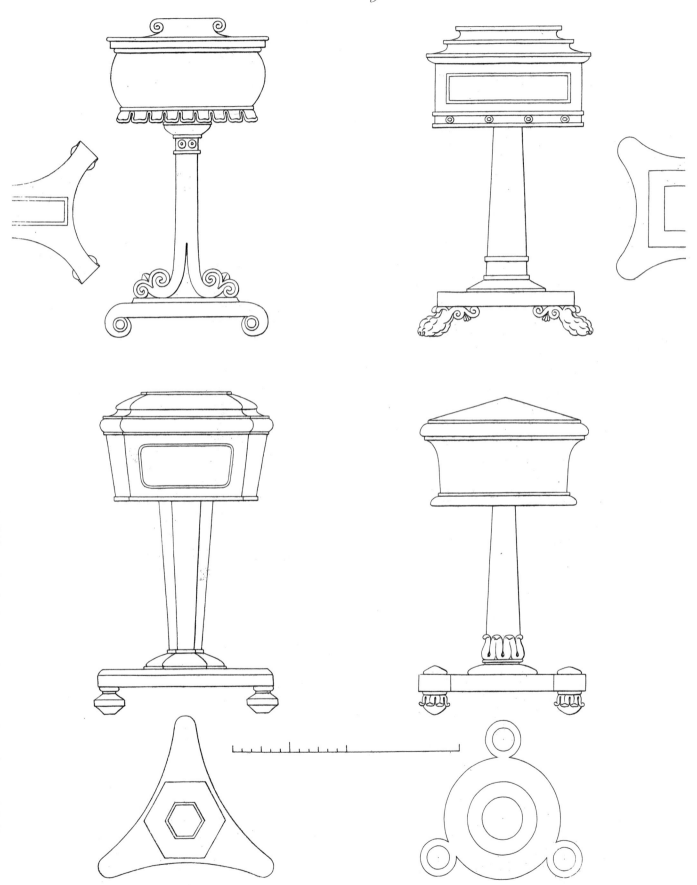

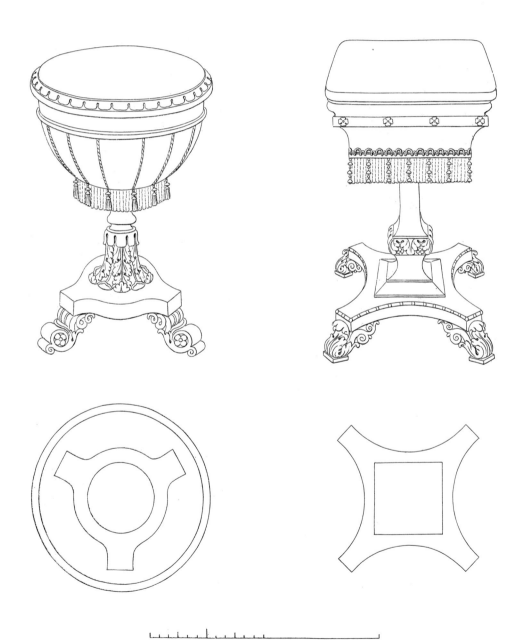

Work Tables.

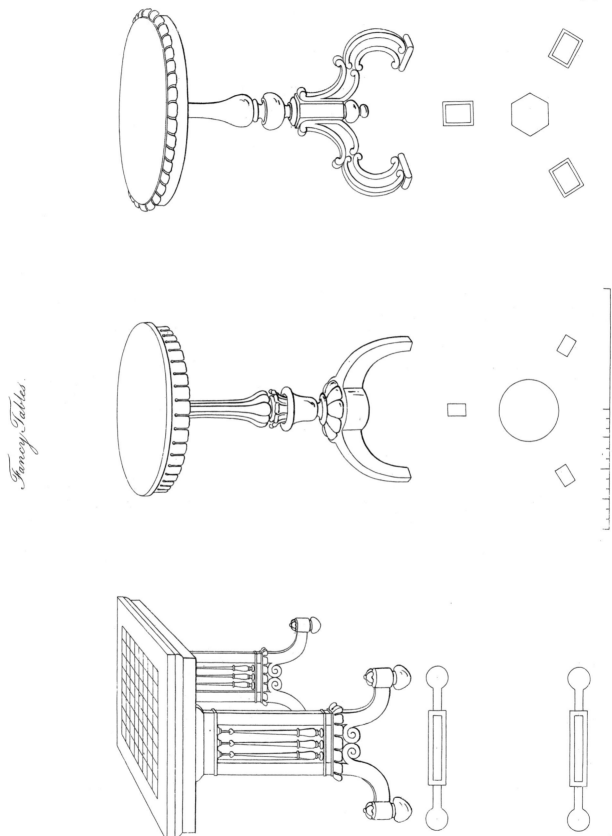

Fancy Tables.

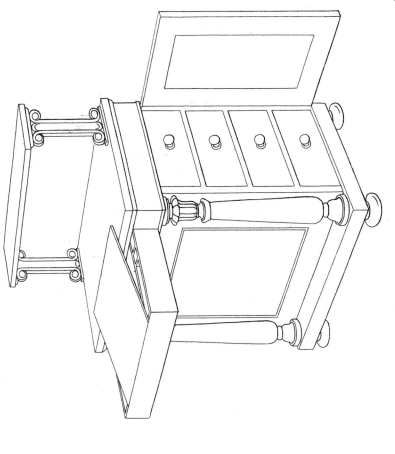

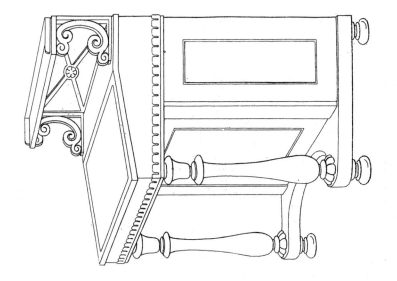

A Gothic Winged Bookcase.

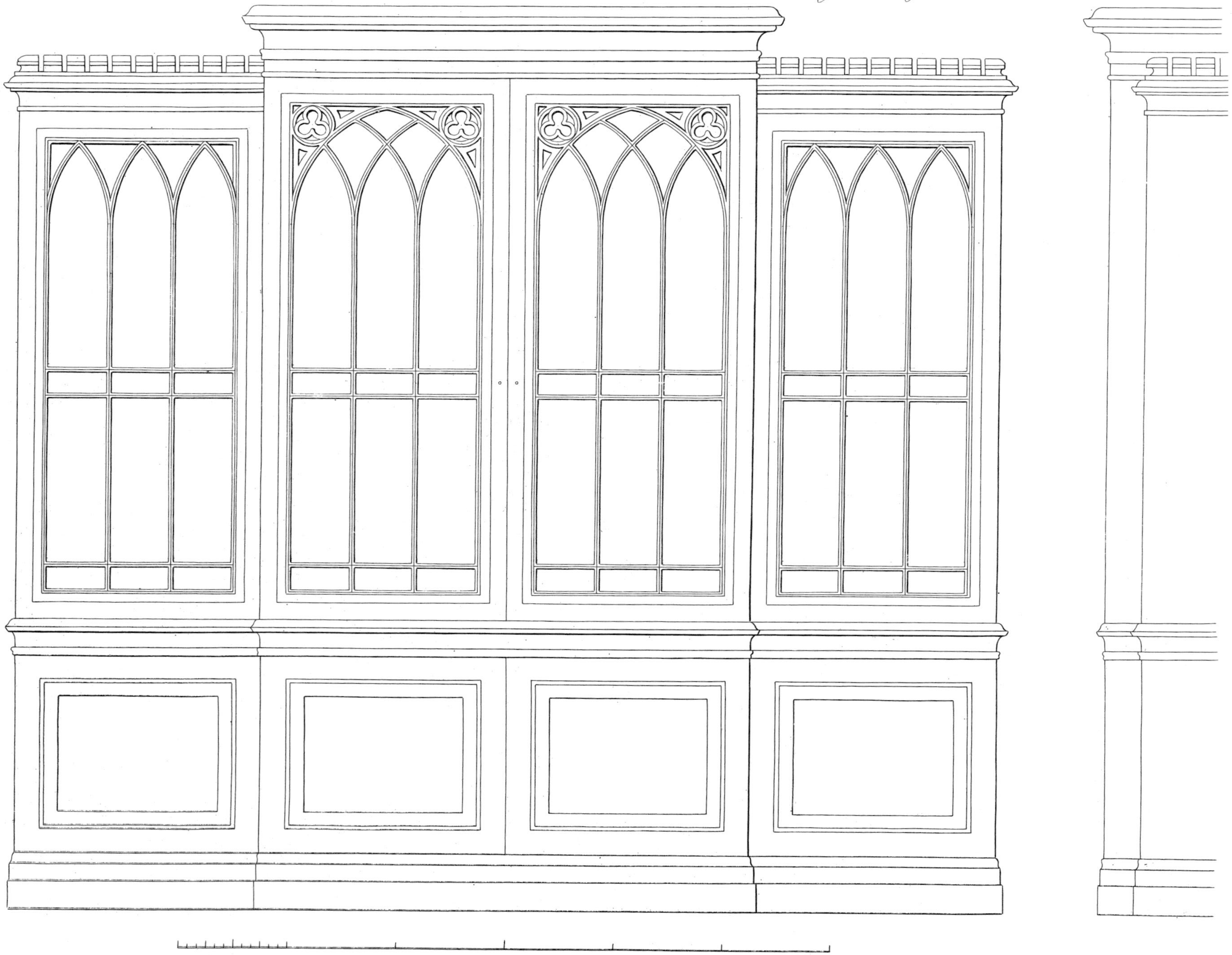

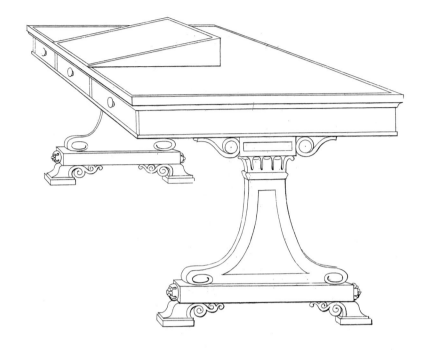

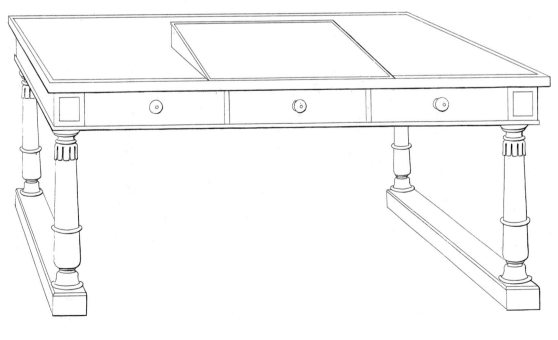

A Toilet.

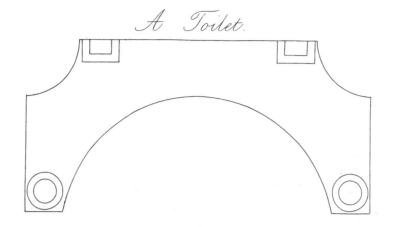

92

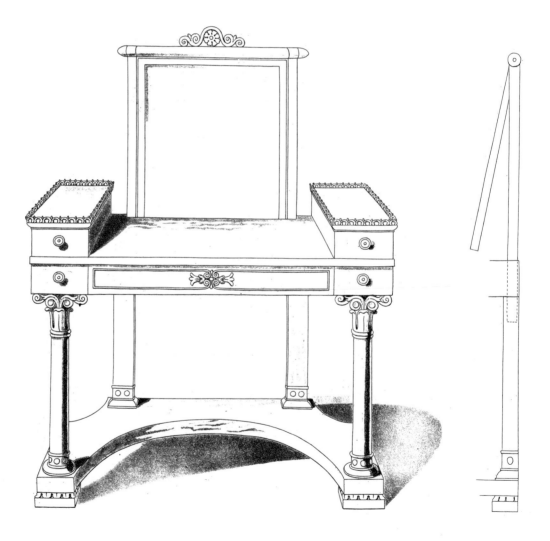

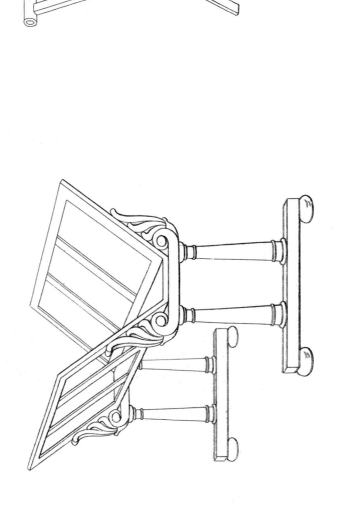

Folio Stands.

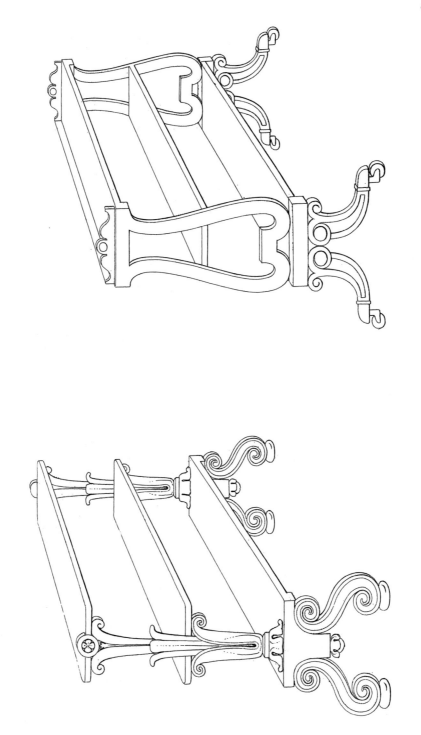

Moving Book Shelves.

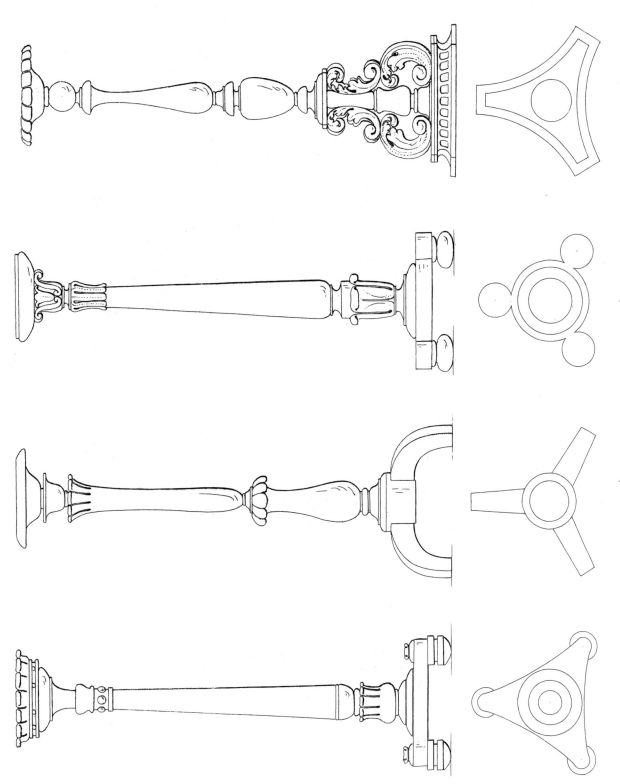

Flower Stands.

French Bedsteads.

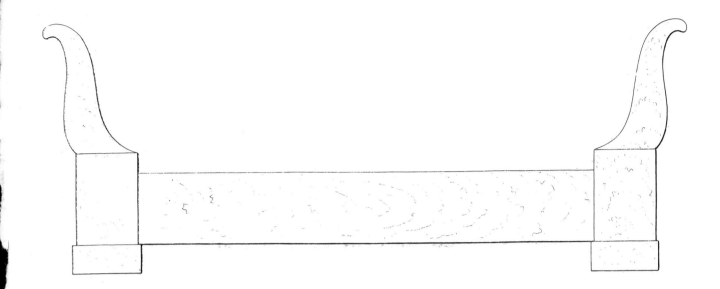

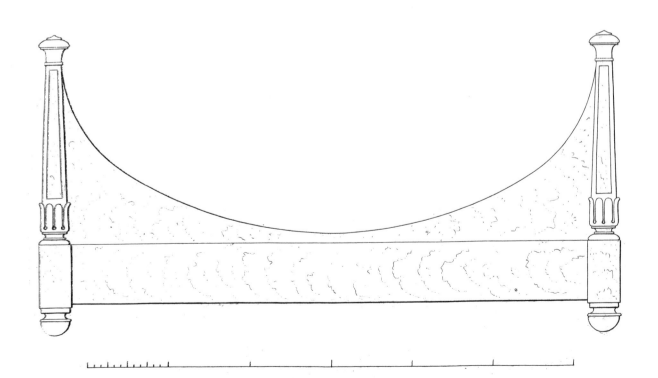

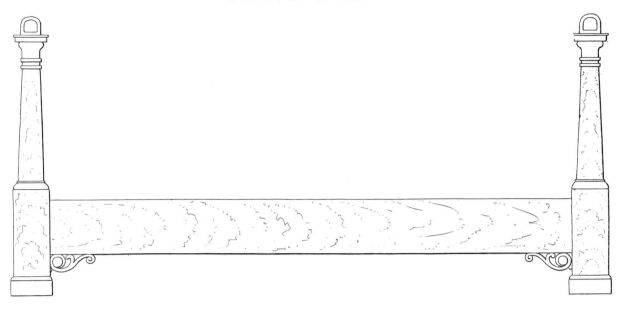

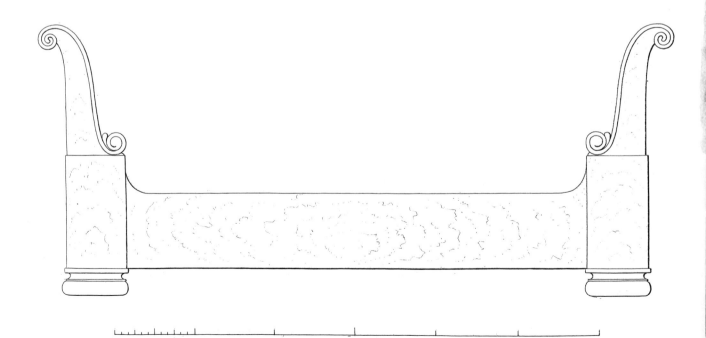

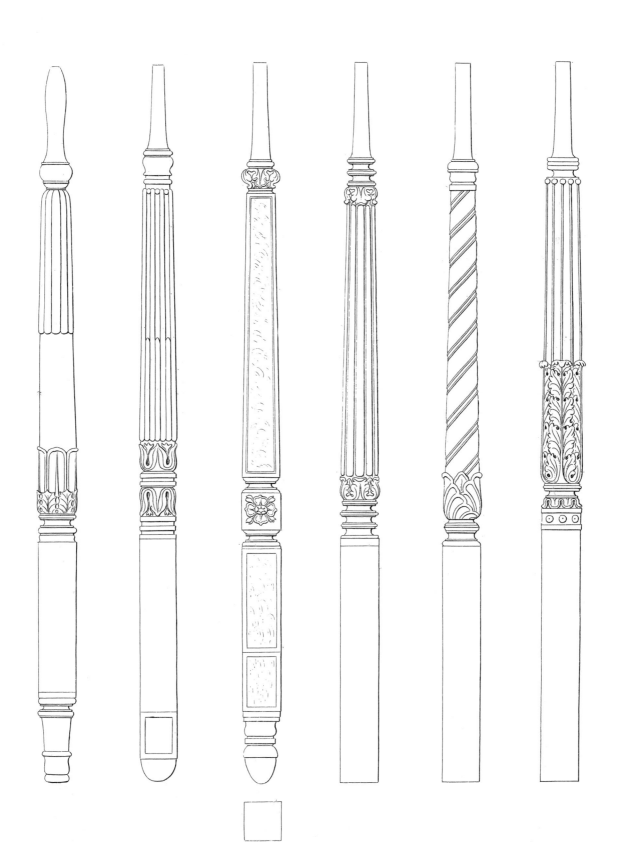

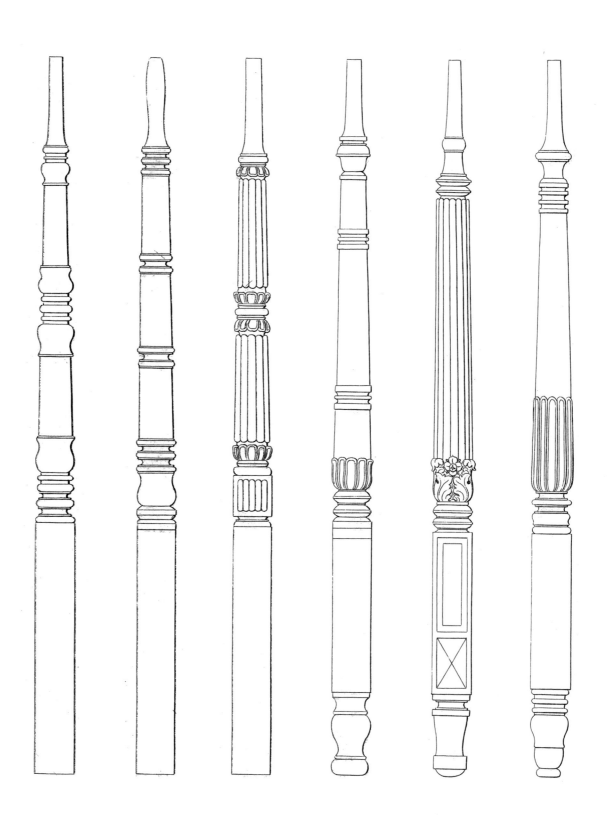